Praise for *Gods at War*

Kyle Idleman knows where we live, and where we could live with God's help. His words are, at once, profound and practical. He is committed to helping us move in the right direction. If you need a helping hand in your journey, he'll point you to the right Person.

> — MAX LUCADO, pastor, Oak Hills Church; author, *Grace*

Kyle will challenge even the most obedient Christians to relook at their relationship with Christ.

> — MIKE HUCKABEE, former governor, Arkansas;
> author, *Dear Chandler, Dear Scarlett*

Pick up this book only if you are weary of losing your battles, if you are done with band-aid solutions, if you are ready for the real winning. You won't finish it and be the same person.

> — ANN VOSKAMP, author, *One Thousand Gifts*

Don't just read this book — read it *now!* Kyle's words will dig deep to expose the false gods that drive us away from the real One. In these pages, liberation awaits.

> — LEE STROBEL, author, *The Case for Christ* and *The Case for Faith*

Kyle Idleman is more of a heart surgeon than an author. He delves deep within each of us and offers practical and biblical advice that can transform the way we wage war in our daily battles.

> — DAVE STONE, senior pastor, Southeast Christian;
> author of the Faithful Families series

Today's false gods are more tempting than ever as they promise comfort, wealth, and happiness. Kyle Idleman equips us to kill the deceitful pests that harass our hearts. Get ready for battle.

> — MARK BATTERSON, pastor, National Community Church;
> author, *The Circle Maker*

Idols are tricky. It's not always easy to identify who or what we place ahead of God. But we still do this every day. *Gods at War* will help you dethrone the idols that rob you of the life God wants you to live.

> — CRAIG GROESCHEL, pastor, LifeChurch.tv; author, *Soul Detox*

Kyle Idleman cuts through all the nonsense and takes us straight to what is most important spiritually. In *Gods at War*, he describes not only what we put before God but how we can put God first again. This engaging and convicting book carries a critically important message for our time.

— JUD WILHITE, senior pastor, Central Christian Church; author, *Pursued*

Praise for *Not a Fan*

Though his message is a direct challenge to the reader, Idleman offers humor and conversation instead of guilt and condemnation. He takes old themes and repackages them with natural wit and twenty-first-century relevance. The meat of this succinct message could be lost if the titular catchphrase becomes yet another T-shirt slogan. But if readers latch onto the deeper meaning, they could find themselves reevaluating everything from their careers to their relationships. A refreshing read to recharge apathetic churchgoers.

— PUBLISHERS WEEKLY

Not a Fan presents an essential, biblical message for people in a culture teaming with fans but lacking in real commitment.

— RELEVANT

Not a Fan does an excellent job of detailing exactly what following Jesus is intended to cost. Discussion of the cost of earnest devotion to Christ is presented in such a way that the appeal is both direct and honest.

— CHRISTIAN BOOK PREVIEWS

Not A Fan is a book that every Christian should read and regularly reread. I started to read the manuscript and could not stop until I finished. This is a NOW message for the church, and my hope is that every believer who reads this will become an authentic follower of Christ.

— CHRISTINE CAINE, founder, The A21 Campaign

gods at war

DEFEATING THE IDOLS THAT BATTLE FOR YOUR HEART

kyle idleman
bestselling author of not a fan.

ZONDERVAN

ZONDERVAN.com/
AUTHORTRACKER
follow your favorite authors

ZONDERVAN

Gods at War
Copyright © 2013 by City on a Hill Studio, LLC

Requests for information should be addressed to:
Zondervan, 3900 *Sparks Dr. SE, Grand Rapids, Michigan* 49546

ISBN 978-0-310-31903-0 (audio)

ISBN 978-0-310-31894-1 (ebook)

Library of Congress Cataloging-in-Publication Data
Idleman, Kyle.
    Gods at war : defeating the idols that battle for your soul / Kyle Idleman.
      p. cm.
    Includes bibliographical references.
    ISBN 978-0-310-31884-2 (softcover)
    1. Idolatry. I. Title.
    BV4627.I34I35 2013
    248.4—dc23   2012042782

Cover design: Curt Diepenhorst
Interior design: Beth Shagene

First printing January 2013 / Printed in the United States of America

To my wife, DesiRae:
Such a gift causes my heart to love the Giver all the more

To Rob Suggs:
Your giftedness is matched only by your humility and grace.
Thank you for your invaluable contributions
and partnership in writing this book.

SDG

contents

introduction

It was just a simple, late-night conversation with my eight-year-old daughter Morgan. But it changed my life and my church.

I was sitting on her bed for our nightly prayers. But she had a surprise for me before we prayed. She had been doing some memory work, and she wanted to recite it for me.

"Dad," she said, "do you want to hear me say the Ten Commandments?!"

"You memorized them all?"

A proud grin came over her face.

"Wow," I said, smiling. "Let's hear them."

I lay down next to her and listened as Morgan worked her way through the greatest top-ten list of them all, the one that came in tablet form and was recorded in Exodus 20.

She made her way through them in her singsong way: "You shall have no other gods before me ... You shall not make for yourself an idol ..."

On down the list. As she finished, my "teachable moment" instincts kicked in. I said, "Morgan, that was great! Let me ask you, have you ever broken any of the commandments?"

She smiled again. This time it wasn't as much a shy smile as a guilty one. Like the smile I give my wife when she asks what happened to the Sour Patch Watermelons that were meant for the kids' lunch boxes. I could see that Morgan was trying to think through an answer that would be honest without indicting her. I decided to help.

"Well let's see," I said, rubbing my chin. "Have you ever lied?" She nodded slowly.

"Have you ever wanted what someone else had so much that you wished they didn't have it?" She nodded, discovering that she was guilty of coveting.

I kept pushing. "I know you haven't murdered anybody, Morgan. But have you ever felt really, *really* angry at someone in your heart? Maybe so much that—just for then—you *hated* that person?"

"Morgan, have you ever, maybe ... oh I don't know ... not honored your father and mother?"

We both knew the answer to that one.

This was not going the way she planned. But hey, that's how it goes when you get stuck with a preacher for a daddy. She let out a heavy sigh, which I immediately recognized. It's the same sigh I get on a Sunday morning when someone is losing interest in the sermon. It was time for me to stop preaching and offer the invitation.

Before I had a chance, her eyes became bright and she said, "Dad, I know one commandment I have never broken! I've never made an idol."

Now, I really, *really* wanted to respond to that!

I wanted to tell my daughter that, as a matter of fact, that particular commandment is the very one we *all* break most often.

I wanted to tell her what Martin Luther said—that you can't violate the other nine without breaking this one first. But as I lay next to my young daughter, I decided it best to save the theology lesson for another day. We prayed and thanked God for sending Jesus to take away our sin and guilt. As I left, I gave her a smile and a kiss on the forehead, and told her I was proud of her for memorizing the Ten Commandments.

But walking down the steps, I wondered how many people see this subject of idolatry exactly as Morgan did. Maybe they see the Ten Commandments as one more checklist, like the rules posted at the community swimming pool — no running by the pool, no diving in the shallow areas, no peeing in the pool. Just a long list of rules. And the one about idols is quickly skipped over because they think they've got that bullet point covered.

After all, the whole subject of idolatry seems mostly obsolete. That command was for then, not now. Right?

As for those thousand or so references to idolatry in the Bible, haven't they expired? We don't know anyone who kneels before golden statues or bows down before carved images. Hasn't idolatry gone the way of leisure suits, shoulder pads, and jelly shoes? Aren't we past all that?

Idolatry seems so primitive. So irrelevant. Is a book on idolatry even necessary? Why not a book about rain dancing and witch doctors?

And yet idolatry is the number one issue in the Bible, and that should raise caution signals for us. Idolatry comes into every book. More than fifty of the laws in the first five books are aimed at this issue. In all of Judaism, it was one of only four sins to which the death penalty was attached.

Seeing my faith and life through the lens of idolatry has rebuilt my relationship with God from the ground up. As we've talked more about it, many in our church would say the same. Understanding the significance of this issue was a game changer.

As we look at life through this lens, it becomes clear that there's a war going on. The gods are at war, and their strength is not to be underestimated. These gods clash for the throne of your heart, and much is at stake. Everything about me, everything I do, every relationship I have, everything I hope or dream or wish to become, depends upon what god wins that war.

The deadliest war is the one most of us never realize is being fought. I understood how my eight-year-old daughter had yet to get a handle on that commandment, but the problem is that most adults haven't done so either. I wonder how many of the rest of us are just where Morgan was, believing they can put a nice checkmark onto that list and dismiss any concern over idols forever. What if it's not about statues? What if the gods of here and now are not cosmic deities with strange names? What if they take identities that are so ordinary that we don't recognize them as gods at all? What if we do our "kneeling" and our "bowing" with our imaginations, our checkbooks, our search engines, our calendars?

What if I told you that every sin you are struggling with, every discouragement you are dealing with, even the lack of purpose you're living with are because of idolatry?

part 1

gods at war

idolatry is the issue

Idolatry is huge in the Bible,
dominant in our personal lives,
and irrelevant in our mistaken estimations.
— Os Guinness

Imagine a man who has been coughing constantly. This cough keeps him up half of the night and interrupts any conversation he has that lasts more than a minute or two. The cough is so unrelenting that he goes to the doctor.

The doctor runs his tests.

Lung cancer.

Now imagine the doctor knows how tough the news will be to handle. So he doesn't tell his patient about cancer. Instead, he writes a prescription for some strong cough medicine and tells him that he should be feeling better soon. The man is delighted with this prognosis. And sure enough, he sleeps much better that night. The cough syrup seems to have solved his problem.

Meanwhile, very quietly, the cancer is eating away at his body.

As a teacher and church leader, I talk to people every week who are ~~coughing~~.

Struggling.

Hurting.

Stressing.

Cheating.

Lusting.

Spending.

Worrying.

Quitting.

Medicating.

Avoiding.

Searching.

They come to me and share their struggles.

They unload their frustrations.

They express their discouragement. They display their wounds.

They confess their sins.

When I talk to people, they point to what they believe is the problem. In their minds, they've nailed it. They can't stop coughing. But here's what I've discovered: they're talking about a symptom rather than the true illness — the true issue — which is always idolatry.

CASE STUDY 1: It's Not about the Money

When I arrive at the office, I see that he's already there, sitting outside my door. I bet he's been there for fifteen minutes. I size him up as the kind of man who has never been late to an appointment in his life.

His clothing and shoes appear to be above my scale. It occurs to me that I should be the one waiting on him, maybe for some kind of high-level business advice. I smile to myself knowing that he's probably thinking the same thing. Still, there is something about him that doesn't match his carefully put together look. What is it that doesn't fit?

There. It's in his eyes. There is deep worry in them, not the easy confidence of the business achiever.

I show him to a seat in my office. He skips the chitchat and gets right to the subject. It's easy to see he's a no-nonsense, get-to-it kind of guy.

"I'm worried about my family," he says with a deep sigh.

"Your family? Is that why you're here?"

"Well, no. It's about me, of course. I just worry about what I've done to them. Their future. Our name."

His story is short and not so sweet. The IRS has caught him cheating on his taxes, on a serious scale. He enumerates the various charges he's facing, and I don't even understand all of them. It's clear that he does, however. And it's clear that, at the very least, he will devote much of the rest of his life to making good on the financial penalties that are soon to be imposed.

I'm not sure what to tell him. He seems to understand the gravity of his situation. I certainly don't give legal advice. But I can see that it's not just about getting caught; it's more about coming to grips with what he has done.

We sit without speaking for a moment, and finally he looks up and says, "The thing I come back to over and over — and can't get an answer to — is why."

"You mean other than financial gain?"

He chuckles drily. "Financial gain? Kyle, I didn't *need* the money. I didn't need a penny of it; I'm a millionaire several times over. I could have gone to my accountants, paid my taxes right down the line, given away plenty more, and still lived the same comfortable life and never known the difference. Whatever I really owed the government? I wouldn't have missed it."

That's a world I don't live in, but I smile and nod, pretending to understand. "Okay. So if not for financial gain, then what's your best 'why' theory?"

His eyes meet mine before wandering to the window. The sun shines on his face, and I can see the slightest hint of wetness in those eyes.

"That's what I'm saying, Kyle. I don't know. I really don't get it. It's ridiculously stupid, and I don't do stupid things. Not with money or anything else. And listen —" He darts a quick look at me. "I know I'm a sinner. I get that. I have no problem calling this what it is: sin. *Ugly* sin. But why *this* sin? Why a sin so unnecessary?"

We talk about it. We talk about his life, his family, his upbringing, and the things that have influenced him. What I want him to see is that sin doesn't just spring up out of nowhere. It usually grows where some kind of seed has been planted.

We need to dig beneath the soil a bit.

"You said the money was unnecessary," I say. "But money, as a rule, has been pretty important for you. Would you agree?"

"Sure. Obviously."

"Important enough that you might describe it as your main motivation, as your master goal?"

He thinks about it. "Yeah. That's fair."

"As a god?"

For a moment he doesn't understand the question. Then he exhales slowly. I see the answer written across his face.

"It wasn't always like that," he says.

"No, it never is, in the beginning. Goals can become gods. You start to serve them, live for them, and sacrifice for them. In the beginning, it was about your money serving you. But at some point, do you think you switched roles?"

"I never thought about it like that."

CASE STUDY 2: No Big Deal

She's a young woman who grew up in our church. Her family wants me to meet and talk with her. They're concerned because she's about to move in with her boyfriend, who isn't a Christian. This ought to be a fun one.

I call her twice and leave messages, but she doesn't return my call. The third time she picks up. She knows why I'm calling and tries to laugh it off.

"I can't believe my parents are making such a big deal out of this," she says with a nervous laugh. I can picture her rolling her eyes. In her mind this whole thing is a mild cough and nothing to worry about.

"Well, I appreciate your talking to me for a few minutes. But I have to ask, do you think it's possible that you've got this backward?"

"What do you mean?"

"That instead of making a big deal out of nothing, it could be that you're making nothing out of a big deal?"

More nervous laughter. "It's not a big deal," she says again.

"Do you mind my telling you why I think it is?"

She sighs deeply and proceeds to give me her prediction of all the reasons she thinks I'll produce.

I interrupt her with a question. "Have you thought about how much moving in together is going to cost you?"

"You mean the cost of the apartment?"

"No, I'm not necessarily talking about money. I mean the way your family feels about it, and the pressure you're getting from them. That's a kind of price, right?"

"Yeah, I guess it is, but that's their problem."

"And what is this going to cost your future marriage?"

"I don't even know if we're going to get married," she responds.

"I'm not necessarily talking about your getting married to him, because statistically speaking, you most likely won't."

She understands what I'm getting at, but I push it a bit farther. "How much is this going to cost your future husband? What price will he have to pay for this decision?" She has to stop and consider that one.

I continue to count the ways that this decision is a big deal, because it's costing her more than she knows.

"So here's what I suggest. If you're willing to pay a price, then this must be pretty important to you. It must be a fairly big deal if you're willing to go through all of this."

I take her silence for reflection, and I finally get to my point. "When I see the sacrifices you are willing to make, and the fact that you are willing to ignore what God has to say about all this, it seems to me that you've turned this relationship into a god."

"What do you mean by that?"

"A god is what we sacrifice for and what we pursue. From where I sit, you have the Lord God on one side saying one thing, and your boyfriend on the other side saying something else. And you're choosing your boyfriend over God. The Bible calls that idolatry, and it's actually a pretty big deal."

No nervous laughter this time. She confesses, "I've never thought about it like that."

CASE STUDY 3: The Secret Struggle

He comes in maybe five or ten minutes late.

He had asked if we could talk for a few minutes, and I suggested meeting for coffee. But he wanted to meet someplace "a little more private." So we set my office as the location.

He arrives and pauses in the doorway, as if still not sure he wants to keep this appointment.

"Come on in." I smile and motion toward a seat.

He answers my smile with a very brief one. He sits, and his body language is all about reluctance. He wraps his arms one around another, lightly massaging his right elbow. I guess he's about my age, midthirties, an ordinary guy. He hasn't told me what this meeting is about, but I know. The conversation I'm about to have has become very familiar.

I ask him a few mundane questions about his work, where he's from, anything to break the ice and create a more relaxed setting. When we've done that for a couple of minutes, he finally broaches his subject. I can tell it takes all the courage he can summon to release his long-held secret.

"I … um … I think I'm addicted to pornography, or something," he stammers.

He looks at his shoes.

"Okay. Well you're not the first person to walk in here and sit in that seat and say those words. How long has this been a struggle?"

He tells his story, starting when he was twelve years old and saw certain images with the guys — in magazines smuggled in from somebody's dad's closet. Pictures that disturbed him at first. Pictures that lodged in his mind, that wouldn't go away, that started calling to him. Pictures he can perfectly visualize all these years later.

He talks about his hatred of the internet. He describes the web as if it were his mortal enemy.

"In the old days, people had to go to those stores," he says. "Ugly stores with the windows all painted over. Cheap, seedy places. I never had the courage to go into one of those stores."

"But the internet is anonymous."

"Exactly," he says. "It's so easy. Any kind of picture, any kind of video is at your fingertips. Just like that. Instant gratification, whenever you feel the slightest urge."

He speaks with the weary tones of a twenty-year slave, of a prisoner who has given up on escape plans.

"What am I supposed to do," he says, "unplug the computer? I'm dependent on the internet like everyone else. I need it for work. I need it for everything. Even if I just used a phone, you can pull up those images there. Turn on the television, and there are a million suggestions. Am I supposed to just watch the Disney Channel?"

He says he had no idea what pornography would do to his life, particularly his relationships. He seems to understand, at least to some degree, how it has changed the way he views and interacts with women.

"Thing is," he said, "you come to see it's just an itch. That's all. An itch. But it never goes away, and you have to scratch. Well, you have to scratch harder and deeper as time goes by. You know what I mean?"

"I know."

There is silence. I'm sure he's expecting me to give the same advice he has heard for so many years: Put a filter on your internet browser. Join a support group. Find an accountability partner. Redirect your eyes. All helpful suggestions, but I know he's tried them all multiple times; otherwise he wouldn't be sitting in front of me.

What I know is that there is an idol that must be dethroned, and until that happens he will suffer. He'll enjoy no intimacy in relationships. He'll struggle to have any real connection with God.

"You think what you have is a lust problem, but what you really have is a worship problem. The question you have to answer each day is, Will I worship God or will I worship sex?"

He doesn't verbalize it, but the expression on his face says, "I've never thought about it like that."

What Lies Beneath

Idolatry isn't just one of many sins; rather it's the one great sin that all others come from. So if you start scratching at whatever struggle you're dealing with, eventually you'll find that underneath it is a false god. Until that god is dethroned, and the Lord God takes his rightful place, you will not have victory.

Idolatry isn't *an* issue; it is *the* issue. All roads lead to the dusty, overlooked concept of false gods. Deal with life on the glossy outer layers, and you might never see it; scratch a little beneath the surface, and you begin to see that it's always there, under some other coat of paint. There are a hundred million different symptoms, but the issue is always idolatry.

That's why, when Moses stood on Mount Sinai and received the Ten Commandments from God, the first one was, "I am the LORD your God, who brought you out of Egypt, out of the land of slavery. You shall have no other gods before me" (Ex. 20:2 – 3). When God issued this command during the time of Moses, the people were familiar with a lot of other gods. God's people had spent more than four hundred years in Egypt as slaves. Egypt was crowded with gods. They had taken over the neighborhood — literally. The Egyptians had local gods for every district. Egypt was the Baskin-Robbins of gods. You could pick and choose the flavors you wanted.

The Bible's paradigm is different. When we hear God say, "You will have no other gods before me," we think of it as a hierarchy: God is always in first place. But there are no places. God isn't interested in competing against others or being first among many.

God will not be part of any hierarchy.

He wasn't saying "before me" as in "ahead of me." A better understanding of the Hebrew word translated "before me" is "in my presence."

God declines to sit atop an organizational flowchart. He *is* the organization. He is not interested in being president of the board. He *is* the board. And life doesn't work until everyone else sitting around the table in the boardroom of your heart is fired. He is God, and there are no other applicants for that position. There are no partial gods, no honorary gods, no interim gods, no assistants to the regional gods.

God is saying this not because he is insecure but because it's the way of truth in this universe, which is his creation. Only one God owns and operates it. Only one God designed it, and only one God knows how it works. He is the only God who can help us, direct us, satisfy us, save us.

As we read Exodus 20, we see that the one true God has had it with the imitation and substitute gods. So God tells the nation of

Israel to break up the pantheon; send it home. All other god activity is cancelled. He makes sure the people understand that he is the one and only. He is the Lord God.

You may be thinking, Thanks for the history lesson, but that was a long time ago. After all, in our time, the problem doesn't appear to be that people worship *many* gods; it's that they don't worship *any* god. Yet my guess is that the list of our gods is longer than theirs. Just because we call them by different names doesn't change what they are. We may not have the god of commerce, the god of agriculture, the god of sex, or the god of the hunt. But we do have portfolios, automobiles, adult entertainment, and sports. If it walks like an idol, and quacks like an idol ...

You can call it a cough instead of calling it cancer, but that doesn't make it any less deadly.

Idol Makeover

One of our problems in identifying the gods is that their identities not only lack the usual trappings of religion; they are also things that often aren't even wrong. Is God against pleasure? Sex? Money? Power?

These things are not immoral but amoral; they are morally neutral until they are not. You could be serving something that is, in itself, very commendable. It could be family or career. It could be a worthy cause. You could even be feeding the hungry and healing the sick. All of those are good things.

The problem is that the instant something takes the place of God, the moment it becomes an end in itself rather than something to lay at God's throne, it becomes an idol. When someone or something replaces the Lord God in the position of glory in our lives, then that person or thing by definition has become our god.

So to identify some gods, look at what you pursue. Another

way to identify the gods at war in your life is to look at what you create.

Remember your commandments.

First: no other gods.

Second: no *making* other gods to worship.

The profound wisdom of that second commandment is that anything in the world can be hammered into an idol, and therefore can be a false god, if misplaced at the top spot of our affections. It's DIY idolatry: choose from our handy assortment of gods, mix and match, create your own.

When God gave Moses the Ten Commandments on Mount Sinai, the people waiting below whined because it was taking so long. Moses had left his brother, Aaron, in charge, and the people began clamoring for a god to lead them. They gathered everyone's gold, put it on the fire, and made a golden calf to worship. A little bit ironic, don't you think? The very moment God was telling Moses about having no other gods before him, the people were down below rigging up a god.

From later in the Bible, here is a reflection on what these people did: "The people made a calf at Mount Sinai; they bowed before an image made of gold. They traded their glorious God for a statue of a grass-eating bull" (Ps. 106:19 – 20 NLT).

That's not a good trade. They traded the Creator God for a god of their own creation.

Are we really any different? We replace God with statues of our own creation.

A house that we constantly upgrade.

A promotion that comes with a corner office.

Acceptance into the fraternity or sorority.

A team that wins the championship.

A body that is toned and fit.

We work hard at molding and creating our golden calves.

I already hear what you're thinking.

"You could say that about anything. You could take any issue, anything someone devoted anything to, and make it out to be idolatry."

Exactly.

Anything at all can become an idol once it becomes a substitute for God in our lives.

To describe the concept more clearly, anything that becomes the purpose or driving force of your life probably points back to idolatry of some kind. Think about what you have pursued and created, and ask yourself, Why?

If you have a food addiction, why?

If you have "hot button" issues that tend to get you upset, why?

If you plan to go shopping this weekend even though you are drowning in debt, why?

If you spend countless hours fixing up the car and redecorating the house, why?

To think of these things as forms of idolatry, we need to use new imagery. Discard the idea of golden cows and multi-armed figurines. Even, just for a moment, strip away the whole idea of idolatry as an item on a ten-point list of don'ts.

This next exercise may seem a bit weird, but stick with me. I want you to reimagine idolatry as a tree.

See it in your mind: one of those great oak trees that seem older than time itself, one with impressive branches reaching out in every direction, branches growing from branches. And when erosion sets in, down the bank or beside the waters, you can see just how deep and far flung its roots are.

Imagine this tree of idolatry with many branches, each with something tied to it.

From one of the branches dangles a pot of gold.

Another branch grows food of all kinds; every delicious food imaginable seems to sprout from a different section of that branch.

Another branch widens into a flat, round ending, and when

you move closer, you can see that it is really a mirror that shows an idealized reflection of yourself.

Yet another branch is carved with beautiful craftsmanship. You follow its sinuous lines and realize it is the image of two human figures, entwined in a sensuous embrace.

One branch has, as fruit, different sets of keys — one set to a luxury car, another to a beach house in Florida.

Quite a peculiar tree. It has many other branches, each one with a curious item attached to it.

Here's the point: idolatry is the tree from which our sins and struggles grow.

Idolatry is always the issue. It's the trunk of the tree, and all other problems are just branches.

chapter 2

the battleground
of the gods

Sometimes very large companies make very bad mistakes.

Remember America Online?* A few years ago, America Online released, to the public, the internet search history of 650,000 of its network users. The company was trying to demonstrate its vast reach among consumers.

An individual's search history meant that if he typed "NFL football scores" into a browser window, it was now a matter of public record.

Already you're saying, "What were they thinking?" But the fact is, AOL had taken certain precautions. No real names were used — only user numbers. So it wasn't Bob down the street, but an anonymous "User #545354," who was checking to see how the Green Bay Packers did.

The problem was that the precautions weren't strong enough. The *New York Times* quickly demonstrated how it was possible to select a user number and put a name to it.

How could they do that? Let's say User #545354 searched for "transmission problems 2002 Chevy Camaro." This wouldn't tell us much on its own, but they also revealed thousands of other

---

* True story: At one point more than 50 percent of the CDs produced worldwide were AOL free software CDs. We collected enough to play Frisbee golf with them when I was in high school.

searches by the same user.* Given enough information it wasn't too difficult to look at the searches and match them up to a specific user.

As you can guess, people didn't simply search for car information or sports scores. They also searched for silly things. Sad things. And many, many truly disturbing things.[1] Each user's "data trail" drew an unflinching picture of that person.

You could say we are defined by our searches.

What would your data trail say about you?

Where does the search you are on lead?

What you are searching for and chasing after reveals the god that is winning the war in your heart. Think of your heart as the battleground of the gods. Your heart is Bunker Hill, where the gods gather and wage war. Whatever god wins the day claims the throne of your heart.

THE SEARCH CONTINUES

Google and several other internet companies track the most searched keywords from day to day, month to month, and year to year. Advertisers, political consultants, and culture watchers pay close attention to what the world is seeking.

At the end of 2011, *Sex* and *video* each logged 338 million searches per month.

Porn: 277 million.

Products and celebrities such as *iPad* or *Lady Gaga* often shoot to the top for short durations.

During a typical period, the singer Justin Bieber was the subject of more searches than God, at more than 30 million searches for Bieber to 20 million for God.*

---

* *www.webupon.com*

---

*Likely searches for a Camaro driver: Metallica, mullet, midlife crisis.

Since I can't check your search history, I want you to examine your heart to find out where your allegiance lies and where your glory goes. "Above all else, guard your heart, for everything you do flows from it" (Prov. 4:23). Your heart defines and determines who you are, how you think, and what you do. Because everything flows from it, your heart is the frontline for the gods at war.

What do we mean when we speak of "the heart"? In science, we know that it's the blood-pumping organ that makes the body run. It doesn't think; it doesn't feel. But in Hebrew culture, the heart was seen differently. It was a metaphor for the center or core of a personality. It was the spiritual hub, and your life flowed from its orientation. The ancients knew that you could lightly touch the wrist and feel a soft beating — what we call a pulse. That same pulse could be felt in the neck and elsewhere. But place the hand over the heart, which is the center of a person, and that beating was more powerful. It stood to reason that everything flowed from the heart — to the Hebrew, not only blood but personality, motives, emotions, and will.

These days, we tend to neatly divide the things that make us human. There's mind over here, body over there — physical and intellectual. But we know better. Science has helped us see that it's all interconnected. Your physical condition affects the way you think and feel; your "spirits" affect your physical health. We have come to see personality more holistically during the last century.

The Hebrews understood that all along. They spoke of loving God with all of your heart, soul, and mind, but they actually understood life as a unified thing — and they spoke of that unity as "the heart." In Hebrew, that word means "the kernel of the nut." Your "heart" reflects your true identity.

Here's an example of the Hebrew idea: "As water reflects the face, so one's life reflects the heart" (Prov. 27:19). The heart is the truth of your identity, that's why the gods fight so fiercely for every inch of it.

The Source

So let's think about your heart, and we'll do it by imagining a scenario. You're out for a hike on a beautiful spring day. You're delighted to hear running water, and sure enough, you come to a creek. But there's something wrong with this picture. You notice that someone has dumped trash into the stream — an ugly sight. There is refuse floating on the water. Judging by some of the empty soda cans, the trash has been there awhile.* And there is an ugly film on the top of the water.

You can't just leave the scene as you found it, because it would bother your conscience. So you stoop down and begin gathering the trash.

It actually takes several hours before you can begin to see a difference; it's amazing how much junk is there. You sit back, rest for a moment, and realize you'll have to keep returning each day until the site is truly clean. Well, that's okay; it's a project you'll be proud of.

Except that when you come back the next day, it's as if your work has been undone.

In fact there's more trash than before. Somehow the garbage bred overnight. You think about the unlikelihood of someone coming to this very spot to dump their garbage in the few hours while you were away, and you realize that something smells fishy — so to speak. So you begin to follow the creek upstream.

Sure enough, you come to a garbage dump that has been there for years. It's emptying into the passing creek. Your cleaning job only opened up a gap for more stuff to settle. You could go and clean every day, but it would just be like pushing a boulder up the hill and watching it roll back down again. Which is surprisingly fun, but, really, what's the point?

---

*Crystal Pepsi and Apple Slice, thanks for the memories. It's not the same without you.

If you want your creek to be clean, that means going directly to the source and dealing with what's there.

Think of your heart, as the Hebrews did, as the source from which your life flows — thoughts, emotions, actions.

How much of your life do you spend dealing with the visible garbage rather than what produces it? We all spend great amounts of time, money, energy, and frustration doing trash removal when something upstream is still dumping into the flow. Even the church focuses downstream too much. It's so much easier to pick up a little bit of trash. Dealing with what's upstream is a staggering commitment. But the gods know the heart is the battlefield. It's where the war is won.

Overlooking the heart and focusing just on what's downstream could be described as "behavior modification." Behavior modification, popularized in mid-twentieth century psychology, is the idea of trying to bring about change by targeting observable and measurable actions. It's symptom-based care, quick-fix methodology.

Here are some examples of how we do trash removal:

- If you have a gambling problem, then stay away from the casino and make it harder to access your accounts.
- If you have an anger problem, then take a deep breath and count to ten.
- If your marriage is in trouble, then schedule some date nights and buy your spouse a gift.
- If you're drowning in debt, then cut up your credit cards.
- If your weight has spiraled out of control, then join a gym and get on a diet.

This is not a condemnation of dieting or nice gifts or cutting up credit cards. All of these things can be positive actions, just as cleaning up the downstream trash is something that must be done. It's simply that the heart of the issue is an issue of the heart.

Walk Upstream

So would you take a few minutes and consider your life? Get past trash removal for a moment and hike upstream to the heart of the problem.

Perhaps there has been a lot of anxiety in your life lately. If you and I were to talk, you might say, "I love the Lord. I don't have any issues with idolatry. My problem is that I just tend to worry too much. I become very anxious."

Okay, but hike upstream. What is it in your heart that is causing all that worry? It could be that if you stopped and examined your heart deeply enough, you would find a deep need to be in control of things. You like every *i* to be dotted, every *t* to be crossed. A place for everything and everything in its place.* You don't like surprises, and you simply want life to go according to script.

No law against any of that, right? As a matter of fact, employers love people like you. They would describe you as highly responsible — someone good with details. But still, you don't enjoy the restless nights, the way the wheels just keep turning in your mind, the fact that you feel no real peace.

The need for control is a relentless god that has taken ground in your heart. In fact the more control you crave, the more that craving will control you, thus making control your god.

Because gods at times form dark alliances of cooperation with each other, maybe the god of control is working with the god of comfort, because yes, your need to cover every detail speaks of a drive to stay as snug within your comfort zone as possible. And so you think the issue is anxiety, while perhaps the real issue is that the gods of control and comfort are winning the war for your heart.

And these gods want to take your life in a much different

---

*Unnecessary and pointless footnotes are irritating. Couldn't agree more.

direction than the Lord God. God is often calling us outside our comfort zones. He's calling us to a great adventure that requires risk and faith. The invitation of Jesus is to take up a cross and follow him. It's hard to carry a cross when comfort is your god. The gods of control and comfort are likely in direct conflict with the Lord God who has called you to a new kind of life.

Let's try another example. What if you come to me and tell me that you are a workaholic? "That's my problem, plain and simple," you say. "I'm a workaholic. How can I stop being one?"

My first impulse is to do some trash removal, so I tell you to pursue the discipline of going home at five o'clock, to leave your work at the office over the weekend, and to find some hobbies to be passionate about. Symptom stuff.

But journey upstream and you'll likely find that being a workaholic isn't really the problem, "plain and simple." There are probably some false gods backstage in your life, creating havoc. What motivations would make someone a workaholic? It could be materialism and the drive for more, more, more. That's definitely an idol.

Or it could be that money isn't really what work is all about for you; you could actually be serving the god of perfectionism. Are you one of those people who is never happy with the results, who thinks it should be done better?

What about the god of power? Maybe you're getting caught up in accumulating as much control as possible because power is important.

Behind all of these, of course, could be that incredibly pervasive god of *me*. I would look at this one very closely. Are you building a monument to your own abilities and personal value through the competence of how you do your work?

It all comes down to what's happening in your heart. And that's why Jesus put so much emphasis there. He wasn't quick to reward good behavior if the heart wasn't right. In Matthew 15:8 Jesus said of the religious leaders, "These people honor me with their lips, but their hearts are far from me." Later in the chapter Jesus says, "Don't you see that whatever enters the mouth goes into the stomach and then out of the body? But the things that come out of a person's mouth come from the heart, and these defile them. For out of the heart come evil thoughts — murder, adultery, sexual immorality, theft, false testimony, slander" (Matt. 15:17 – 19).

We want to focus on the outside, but Jesus makes the point that it's all about what's inside. The heart is the battleground for the gods because everything flows from it.

I was talking to a friend of mine who is a cardiologist. He was telling me about a procedure called an arteriogram that is used to diagnose how healthy a heart is. Here's how it works: He injects a dye into the bloodstream, then an X-ray is taken of the arteries to locate any blockages. Once they locate a blockage, he will insert a stent through the patient's leg and open up the blood vessel.

But what is interesting is that frequently a heart problem goes undetected and undiagnosed for years. No arteriogram is done to test the heart. Why? Because the symptoms don't seem relevant. A patient may face insomnia, back pain, a loss of appetite, anxiety, vision problems, and other challenges. But the patient seeks medical help to treat the *symptoms*. They think they have a sleeping issue or a back pain issue or a vision issue, when in truth it's a heart issue. It's cardiovascular, and until that is addressed, the patient isn't going to get better.

A Spiritual Arteriogram

It's difficult to see ourselves as idol worshipers. Whatever our symptoms might be, we struggle to connect them to the throne of the heart and what occupies it. But that is where the battle is being fought. So I want to ask you to do a spiritual arteriogram to discover your heart health. I'm going to ask you a series of questions that only you can answer.

Think of these questions as dye being injected into your bloodstream that will help reveal and locate some problem areas.

What Disappoints You?

When we feel overwhelmed by disappointment, it's a good sign that something has become far more important to us than it should be. Disproportionate disappointment reveals that we have placed intense hope and longing in something other than God.

So if you were to identify your greatest disappointments, where would you point? The realm of career? The lives of your children? Your marriage or your sex life? Erwin Lutzer writes, "Have you ever thought that our disappointments are God's way of reminding us that there are idols in our lives that must be dealt with?"[2]

What Do You Complain about the Most?

This question is similar to the last, but we're looking at the outside this time — what you express. This might be a good time to get an objective opinion. Ask someone close to you about your typical complaints.

If you constantly complain about your financial situation, maybe money has become too important to you.

If you constantly whine to your spouse about your sex life, maybe sexual pleasure has become a god.

If you constantly complain about a lack of respect in the office, maybe what other people think about you matters more than it should.

If you constantly complain about what kind of year your team is having, maybe sports has become your god.

What we complain about reveals what really matters to us. Whining shows what has power over us.

Whining, in many ways, is the opposite of worshiping the Lord. Worship is when we glorify God for who he is and acknowledge what he has done for us, but whining is ignoring who God is and forgetting what he has done for us.

Where Do You Make Financial Sacrifices?

More on this later, but the Bible says where your treasure is, that's where your heart is also. Where your money goes shows what god is winning your heart. So take a look at your bank statements and credit card bills, and pretend that you are examining the spending habits of a perfect stranger to find out what is most important to them.

What Worries You?

It could be the idea of losing someone significant, or losing your job or house or talent. It could be the fear of being ridiculed. Maybe it's the fear of being alone. You can care so deeply about something that it has a hold on you deep inside and is revealed when your mind is in free form mode at night. Whatever it is that wakes you — or for that matter keeps you up — has the potential to be an idol.

Where Is Your Sanctuary?

Where do you go when you're hurting?

Let's say it's been a terrible day at the office. You come home and go — where? To the refrigerator for comfort food like ice cream? To the phone to vent with your most trusted friend? Do you seek escape in novels or movies or video games or pornography? Where do you look for emotional rescue?

The Bible tells us that God is our refuge and strength, our help in times of trouble — so much so that we will not fear though the mountains fall into the heart of the sea (Ps. 46:1 – 2). That strikes me as a good place to run. But it's so easy to forget, so easy for us to run in other directions. Where we go says a lot about who we are. The "high ground" we seek reveals the geography of our values.

When I was interviewed for my current ministerial position, the elders of the church asked me various questions. One seemed particularly important to them: Tell us about your sufferings and hardships.

I thought about it and came up with a challenge or two I'd faced, but had to admit I'd never really suffered. One of the elders was concerned about that response. I thought, What am I supposed to do? Go lose a loved one?

Since he kept pushing the issue, he finally explained, "You don't know who people really are until they've suffered."

A few weeks later, I came home from work and went upstairs to awaken Morgan from her nap. She was two at the time. I saw that her five-foot-tall pine dresser had fallen over, and then I realized she was under it. My heart almost stopped. I frantically moved the furniture and saw that my daughter was black and blue.

We rushed her to the hospital, and there was a flurry of tests and X-rays. Nothing was broken. She was breathing but unresponsive. Nerve damage was likely. I remember sitting in that dark hospital hall as they took her in for the initial X-rays. I was on the floor with my back against the wall, crying and praying. I began to sing, "Our God Is an Awesome God."

A week later, though my daughter was awake, she was unable to walk. Her left leg just wouldn't move. I kept praying, clinging to God, and as time went on, she improved. She's fine these days, but I realized along the way that the elder had been right. I needed to learn something about myself, see how things would be between God and me when life got hard.

I discovered he would be my sanctuary even if my deepest fears were realized.

What Infuriates You?

Everyone has a hot button or two — something that we say "makes us crazy." Are you so competitive that you can't stand for your team to lose a pickup game at the gym? Could it be that being the best is your idol? How do you respond sitting in traffic? When someone cuts you off, drives too close, speeds up and won't let you in, why does this stranger have so much power over your emotions? What about when someone embarrasses you or doesn't treat you with respect? What's the real issue here? Maybe your quick temper reveals the oldest idol of them all — the god of me.

What Are Your Dreams?

If nightmares are revealing, so are daydreams — the places we *choose* for our imagination to go. What fantasy has a grip on you and puts a twinkle in your eye? Do you dream of being the next American Idol, or maybe a first-round draft pick? Aspirations are fine, but the question is why you aspire to those things.

Is your motivation to give God glory or is your motivation your own glory, fame, and fortune?

chapter 3

a jealous god

Michael Jordan's book *Driven from Within* tells an eye-opening story about a visit the legendary basketball player made to a friend's home. Fred Whitfield was the president and chief operating officer of another NBA team. The two of them were getting ready to go out to dinner when Jordan said, "Man, it's kind of cold. Can I borrow one of your jackets?"

Whitfield said, "Sure," and told him where the coat closet was.

Jordan disappeared down the hall, and the house fell silent for a moment. Then the star reappeared, carrying an armful of branded athletic jackets, shirts, shoes, and other gear. He dumped the whole pile on the floor and disappeared down the hall again for more.

Whitfield looked at the heap and noted that all the items were made by Puma, a rival of Nike. Jordan had found that the closet had materials made by both manufacturers, and Jordan, so associated in the public mind with the Nike swoosh, did not approve. The Nike items were there because Whitfield was a close friend of Michael Jordan. The Puma stuff had come as the result of his close friendship with Ralph Sampson, an ex-player who promoted that brand.

Whitfield stood and waited to see the fate of his Puma gear. Jordan walked into the kitchen, came out with a butcher knife, and cut the pile of gear on the floor into thousands of pieces.

When he had thoroughly destroyed the athletic gear, he gathered it all up again and carried it to a dumpster for disposal.

When he was done, Jordan returned to Whitfield's side and said, "Hey, dude, call [my Nike representative] tomorrow and tell him to replace all of this. But don't ever let me see you again in anything other than Nike. You can't ride the fence."[3]

Jordan's behavior is a little uncomfortable to read about, isn't it? I find that people who follow Christ, people who read books like this one, are *polite* people. I can't imagine myself pulling a Michael Jordan in someone's house, nor would I recommend it to those who wish to keep their friends.

But don't you think Jordan offers us a pretty good picture of idol smashing? He is demonstrating total commitment. And really that's the kind of radical commitment God longs for from his people. He doesn't want us to just make room in our closet for him; he wants the closet to himself.

Already we detect a problem. What has come to be called the "Greatest Generation" — the one that fought the Second World War and built mid-century America — is a generation known for commitment. Many of us had grandparents or perhaps great-grandparents who worked one job, lived in one home, and attended one church for the duration of their adulthood. People were committed to companies, communities, congregations, and their families.

In our times, it's common to live a nomadic existence, to move from city to city, from church to church within cities, from partner to partner. Our eyes are always on the horizon, looking for the bigger house, the superior career choice, the better life. We're always watching for a better deal. We live in a world where "no strings attached" is a popular choice when it comes to relationships. We seem to be a generation with one commitment: keeping our options open.

While keeping our options open is not necessarily all bad, we should recognize that this quality that seems to mark our culture makes it that much more difficult to appreciate the seriousness of idolatry. The only relationship God is interested in is one that is exclusive and completely committed. He is not interested in an "open relationship" with you. He won't consider sharing space on the loveseat of your heart.

His throne has only one seat.

Hey Jealousy . . .

You shall not make for yourself an [idol] in the form of anything. . . . You shall not bow down to them or worship them; for I, the LORD your God, am a jealous God.
— Exodus 20:4–5

Wouldn't it be interesting if people were not only called by their given names but also by their most dominant personality traits? Wives, what would your husband's name be? Maybe something complimentary like *sweet-talker* or *strong protector*. Or maybe it would be something a little less complimentary.*

In Scripture, the Lord God is often named by his character qualities. He is the "King of Kings," "Deliverer," "Provider," "Healer," and "Redeemer"; the list goes on and on. Yet of all the names of God, there is one that seems out of place. Exodus 34:14 reads, "Do not worship any other god, for the LORD, whose name is Jealous, is a jealous God."

Jealous? That word doesn't seem very . . . well, *positive*. If feels petty to me — like a couple of junior high girls who are both interested in the same boy; like a basketball player who avoids passing the ball to the teammate who keeps getting the high score; like a possessive high school boyfriend who becomes upset if his girlfriend makes eye contact with another guy.

---

* Cheapskate, time waster, belly itcher.

Besides, what reason would God have to be jealous? Doesn't everything already belong to him? Is there anything that competes with his power or his greatness? Of course not — at least not in reality.

But what about in your heart?

God is jealous for your heart, not because he is petty or insecure, but because he loves you. The reason why God has such a huge problem with idolatry is that his love for you is all-consuming. He loves you too much to share you.

Paul Copan, a philosophy professor at Palm Beach Atlantic University, asks the question, When can jealousy be a good thing?

He describes God's deep passion for our wholehearted devotion. People, he says, are like the dog who drinks out of the toilet

---

IDOLS AND ICONS

Neurologists study the brain. A group of them scanned the brains of religious folk as they discussed the times they've felt God's presence most intimately. They exposed the same people to stimuli such as stained glass, incense, or religious imagery, and discovered that the *caudate nucleus*, an area of the brain, responded when those people felt close to God. (This *isn't* the area, by the way, that has been identified as the "God spot" in recent news stories.)

The neurologists tested another group of people. They got away from the subject of religion, but showed these other people images of consumer goods connected to very popular brands.

Again, the caudate nucleus lit up!

The conclusion: consumers who buy certain well-marketed items have something close to a religious experience.[*]

---

[*] James Bryan Smith, *The Good and Beautiful Life* (Downers Grove, IL: InterVarsity, 2010), 163–64.

bowl and says, "It doesn't get much better than this!" We could be enjoying the living water that only Christ can offer, yet we choose substitutes that are shockingly, disgustingly inferior. God knows what he has in mind for us, and it grieves him to see the choices we make in ignorance. It makes him jealous, in the most righteous and loving way.

Copan writes, "A wife who doesn't get jealous and angry when another woman is flirting with her husband isn't really committed to the marriage relationship.... Outrage, pain, anguish — these are the appropriate responses to such deep violation. God isn't some abstract entity or impersonal principle.... We should be amazed that the Creator of the universe would so deeply connect himself to human beings that he would open himself to sorrow and anguish in the face of human rejection and betrayal."[4]

And here's what is said of God: "For the LORD your God is a consuming fire, a jealous God" (Deut. 4:24).

In the Bible, the words *jealous* and *zealous* are basically interchangeable — it's the same Hebrew word in the original texts. In English, we spell the two almost the same because they derive from the same Greek root. We think of *zeal* as being intense enthusiasm. That idea captures why God is so possessive about us: he is, as he says, a consuming fire of passion for us.

Do you remember falling deeply in love — how you burned with a deep passion for the love of someone, how you were consumed with these feelings? That was only the barest shadow of the power of God's love for you. We need to remember, as we talk about God's intolerance of idolatry, that everything comes back to a passionate love that is so immense, so powerful, that it burns hotter than a billion suns.

I hope you'll think about that as you read this book, because here is what will happen. As we walk through the temples of the modern gods in these pages, you'll recognize the ones that are at war in your life. And God will speak. He'll challenge you with two words: you choose.

You choose between me and money.

You choose between me and your career.

You choose between me and that relationship.

You choose between me and the house.

If you keep watch over your own heart, you'll face those dichotomy moments, those fork-in-the-road moments. He won't give you the option of making him one of many. There is no room there for anyone or anything but himself. That's how much he loves you.

Idolatry Is Adultery

The prophet Ezekiel used a powerful analogy to describe what idolatry feels like to God. He compares it to a cheating spouse. This analogy runs all through the Scriptures. In the New Testament, the church is described as the bride of Christ, and many of Jesus' parables revolve around a bride being faithful as she awaits her bridegroom.

The pain of having an unfaithful partner is surely one of the most agonizing human experiences. It's the ultimate betrayal. Yet this is how we are described when we reject the love of God for cheap substitutes. God is the betrayed lover.

As I discussed this concept with our church, I asked them to imagine going to a local restaurant and seeing me having a romantic candlelight dinner with a woman who is not my wife. Then, I said, imagine walking up and asking me who I was with and what it was all about.

Picture me smiling nonchalantly and saying, "Oh, I'm on a date!"

"But what about your wife?"

"What about her? I love her too. I've taken her out plenty of times."

I'm pretty sure you'd walk away angry and disgusted, and you'd have good justification.

Can you imagine my wife, afterward, meeting me at the door with a big smile? She would say, "Hi, honey. Did you have a good time on your date?"

News flash: this would not happen.

Her hurt, her anger, and her pain would be enormous. And in fact, I would be offended if she *didn't* feel that way. If she was anything other than jealous, it would show me that she didn't really care.

It's overwhelming to realize that the Lord God loves us this way; it changes the way we see ourselves. Everything in life has more significance when someone loves you like that — especially God himself.

And he does, of course. He isn't happy to be one of many gods that we worship. He makes it clear that we are to love him with all our heart, soul, mind, and strength. That statement is often given as the positive summary of the Ten Commandments. The negatively stated summary would be this: "You will have no other gods before me." There is no cohabitation. There is no open marriage.

Hot Pursuit

The jealousy of God is demonstrated not just in the offense he takes at our idolatry, but in his pursuit of our hearts. He doesn't just let you run off with some lover; he relentlessly chases after you. No matter what god seems to be winning the war for your heart at this moment, you can be sure of one thing — the one true God will not give up without a fight. God is in pursuit of our wandering, adulterous hearts, and he will stalk us to our graves.

The poet Francis Thompson produced some unlikely imagery for this idea when he wrote a famous piece called "The Hound of Heaven." Thompson was a Christian who led a very troubled life.

He had health problems, financial problems, and an addiction to opium, which was a legal but dangerous substance in his time. We can guess at some of the false gods he pursued.

As he looked at the turmoil of his life, he kept expecting to find that God had turned his face away in disgust. After all, Thompson had made such a mess of everything; surely the Lord had abandoned such an unworthy servant. Yet somehow, in the deepest of Thompson's suffering, there was always the sense of God's presence, God coming after him, God attempting to rescue him from himself.

In the poem, Thompson wrote,

> I fled Him, down the nights and down the days;
> I fled Him, down the arches of the years;
> I fled Him, down the labyrinthine ways
> Of my own mind; and in the mist of tears
> I hid from Him.

He describes the relentless pursuit of the Hound of Heaven: the sound of divine footfalls behind him, the unhurried pace of the patient hunter, the voice that continues to remind him that there can be no other god, no other sanctuary. His love is more jealous, more zealous, than our stubborn resistance. God kept tracking him like a hound after a fox.

If someone ever asks you, "What's so special about Christianity? What sets it apart from Buddhism, Hinduism, Islam, or anything else?" your answer is found right here. Nowhere else do we find God in hot pursuit of people.

God is imagined in countless ways on this planet. Maybe he lives on Mount Olympus, as the Greeks thought, and comes to earth only occasionally, when he's bored. Maybe "he" is actually an entire pantheon of gods, as the Hindus have it; maybe there are so many of them that you need a scorecard to keep track. Maybe *God* is just another word for nature, as the pantheists believe, meaning that the tree outside my window is God; this chair is God; hey, you and I are God! Maybe there *is* no God as such, as the Buddhists have it; the answers are supposedly within us.

Christianity offers a view of God that is strikingly different from any other. In Christianity, there is one God. He is all-powerful. He takes an active role as father to every human being. His most striking feature is not anger or power or transcendence or even creativity but instead is his relentless, all-consuming love. No one would have just *made up* such a God. The idea is too outrageous.

This is a God who comes from heaven, from all of his perfection and purity and might, to us, in all of our weakness and impurity, and puts on skin, taking the form of a helpless baby all in pursuit of your heart. This is God who, when turned down, ignored, rejected—even violently, even blasphemously—finds a new way to express his love and issue the invitation. This is a God who has never given up on winning your heart. Never.

You can't understand the seriousness of idolatry without understanding the jealousy of God. And you can't understand his jealousy without some understanding of his relentless, powerful love for you, because they are intertwined.

The entire Bible is a love letter to humanity in the form of a story, so that we'll see what God has seen since he first created us; so that we'll know all the ways we've insulted his love and all the ways he has redoubled his pursuit. This is a God who gives us the freedom to say no but insists on giving us every possible, conceivable chance to say yes. He has been called "The Hound of Heaven" because he never gets off the trail.

The Old Testament is a story of our foolish, self-destructive rebellion as God's people. He offers us a special relationship, and time after time we take his gifts and turn away, choosing one idol or another instead of the amazing opportunity he has for us. By the end of the Old Testament, people have turned so far away from

God that heaven seems silent. There are no more prophets. There is no more deliverance from enemies. God seems to have abandoned the human race, though in truth it's just the opposite.

And then God, in the deepest and most startling expression of his relentless pursuit, sends his own Son. God is back, and this time, it's personal—not that it hasn't always been for him. But now God has put everything on the line. He has given his one and only Son. Being God, and knowing all things, he knew exactly how it would come out. He knew about the arrest, the unfair trial, the beatings, the mocking, the crucifixion.

The event of the coming of Jesus represents just how far God is willing to go to win your heart. He had to make a choice, a choice between your heart and the life of his Son. "God so loved the world that he gave his one and only Son" (John 3:16).

Can you feel him coming after you? Can you hear his footfalls? Can you feel the whisper that says, "I will not take no for an answer"?

In Charles Dickens's novel *David Copperfield*, a family lives by the sea in an old, abandoned boat. The father figure, who is an aging, long-retired fisherman, has an adopted nephew and niece that live with him. The niece is named Emily, and he dotes on her. His greatest aspiration is to see her married and happy with a fine young man.

But Emily has other ideas. She is taken in by a fast-talking, handsome man who promises to marry her and show her the great sights of the world, if she'll run away with him that night. She does, but it soon becomes clear that he has no intention of marrying her. And, since this is the mid-1800s, her name is ruined, and the name of her humble family is ruined. It was understood in such situations that someone who messes up on this scale shouldn't even think about going home. A young lady has no recourse but prostitution. And that's what happens to Emily.

Her grief-stricken uncle understands all this, but it makes no difference. He takes every penny to his name and leaves to search the entire world for his niece. If that takes the rest of his life, so be it. He will visit every dark, seedy street corner in every town in Europe until he finds her, because his love for her is completely unaffected by what she has done. He simply can't stand to lose her. So he searches for many years, until all his hairs gray. Finally he locates her and brings her home. She can't believe he had come searching for her; she can't believe anyone would care about her. But he is happier than he has ever been, because his child has come home.

Jesus told a similar story, this time about a prodigal son who left and whose father ran out to meet him when he returned. That's our God — our jealous, insistent, loving God. While we were yet sinners, Christ died for us. While we were yet sinners, God kept coming. And he still does. He is doing so in my life and in yours. He hates everything that becomes an obstacle between you and him, everything that blocks your view of him or threatens to keep you from hearing his voice. He wants you, and not just some of you.

He is jealous for your whole heart.

chapter 4

calling all gods

Kylie Bisutti knew exactly what goals she was pursuing. She wanted to be a fashion model, and she succeeded at the highest level. In 2009, Bisutti won a competition against ten thousand rivals in the Victoria's Secret Model Search. Victoria's Secret, of course, is an American lingerie retailer, a five billion dollar business. It's known for its fashion show, its catalogues, and of course its "angels," who are the models it routinely transforms into fashion icons.*

"Victoria's Secret was my absolute biggest goal in life," she said. "It was all I ever wanted career-wise. I actually loved it while I was there."

Just before her dreams came true, Bisutti had gotten married. She and her husband were followers of Christ, and she couldn't help but think about what she was doing and the example she was setting. She realized there was a great deal of difference between modeling clothing and flaunting provocative undergarments.

She came to the conclusion that her body was for her husband to see, and not for millions of voyeurs on the internet. She also realized she cared deeply about the legions of young Christian girls who looked up to her. She worried that it would be so much easier for them to begin choosing skimpy, suggestive clothing because of her example.

---

*So I've been told.

There was something else too. "I finally achieved my biggest dream," she said, "the dream that I always wanted. But when I finally got it, it wasn't all that I thought it would be."

Stop. Go back. Read that sentence again. You're not gonna do it, are you? Then let me give it to you again: "I finally achieved my biggest dream," she said, "the dream that I always wanted. But when I finally got it, it wasn't all that I thought it would be." How many times have we heard that one? Someone has a dream. They yearn for it; they reach for it; they give all they have to attain it; and it doesn't measure up.

Her greatest goal was unmasked as just another god that couldn't deliver.

Kylie Bisutti's dreams had come true, only for her to come to the conclusion that they were the wrong dreams, even if millions of other women shared them. She knew that following Jesus and giving glory to the Lord God meant turning away from the gods that so many people spend their lives bowing down to. Ultimately it became a worship choice. So she turned in her wings and stepped down from lingerie modeling.[5]

Have you ever had a moment like the one she had, when you realized you had to make a choice, and that your entire future hinged on the choice you made? That if you took a certain kind of job, made a certain ethical decision, pursued a certain life partner, then the ramifications for your future would be immense?

Sometimes we stand at those forks in the road, and we know exactly what's at stake with the decision that must be made. But so many other times, we just keep walking, wandering down a particular path without really thinking about it. We make many choices without even being aware that we are choosing. We do things because that's the way our family has always done them. Or because that's the way certain other people, people we admire, do them. Or because these days almost everyone does them that way.

Whether or not we are aware of it, it turns out that just like

Kylie Bisutti, we regularly make choices that declare which gods are winning the war in our lives.

Doors 1, 2, and 3

Moses led the homeless nation of Israel out of Egypt, where the people had been enslaved for several generations. God demonstrated his power through the ten plagues, the splitting of the Red Sea, and the provision of food from heaven and water from a rock. He even provided them with a supernatural GPS system by leading them with a cloud during the day and a pillar of fire at night.

But the people still didn't have much faith. They constantly whined and complained. It should have been about a month-long hike to the Promised Land, but God caused them to wander in the wilderness for nearly forty years. This was basically a camping trip that lasted four decades. Moses and his generation died before entering the land God had promised Abraham hundreds of years earlier. Joshua replaced Moses as the leader of God's people and brought them into the Promised Land.

By the time we come to Joshua 24, Joshua himself has become an old man; he's pushing 110. He has led a life of great faith. For example, twelve spies were dispatched into Canaan to scout the land. Ten came back and said, "No way can we pull this off; those are giants in there." Joshua was one of only two who discounted any opposition, as long as God was present. He and Caleb trusted the Lord and feared nothing.

At this part of the story, Joshua has been a general through many wars. He has fought off hostile tribes who sought to destroy the Israelites. He has seen the walls of Jericho come thundering down in miraculous fashion. He has fought the battles, and he bears the scars as well as the wisdom and faith that grows and deepens with the struggle.

Joshua seems to know he doesn't have much time left in this

world. He gathers the people of Israel together for what he must
see as a farewell address. He stands and clears his throat as the
assembly turns toward him in expectancy. He's no longer the powerful figure he once was, but still his voice carries power: "Now
fear the LORD and serve him with all faithfulness. Throw away
the gods your ancestors worshiped beyond the Euphrates River
and in Egypt, and serve the LORD. But if serving the LORD seems
undesirable to you, then choose for yourselves this day whom you
will serve, whether the gods your ancestors served beyond the
Euphrates, or the gods of the Amorites, in whose land you are
living. But as for me and my household, we will serve the LORD"
(Josh. 24:14 – 15).

Joshua doesn't tiptoe around what he wants to say. He gets
right to the point and throws down a challenge: it's time for the
people to make a choice. The people can follow the Lord God, the
God of Abraham, Isaac, and Jacob, or they can choose a different
god. It's time to select a god and follow him, to accept a worldview
and allow it to remake them.

"It's up to you," Joshua is saying. "But I can tell you this much.
As for me and my house, our decision is made. We know whom we
will serve; but you must make your own choice."

As a preacher I find it interesting that Joshua gives three other
options along with the one true God. When I offer an invitation to
salvation, I don't make it multiple choice. But even though Joshua
is a commander, a general used to giving orders, he knows that a
choice must be made. No one can be ordered into the kingdom
of God. No one can be driven there or carried bodily over the
threshold. It's a path that individuals must choose, at the expense
of all other paths.

So Joshua lays it out. He shows the people what's behind the
other three doors. He breaks it down this way:

• Follow the *old* gods from beyond the river, from the place
  where you started out.

- Follow the gods you met *next*, in Egypt, where you were enslaved.
- Follow the *local* gods, those of the people recently defeated by the one true God.

At first blush, we read that and think, No problems for me. I don't worship Egyptian or "local" gods, or any from "beyond the river." But forget the details for a moment, and notice that each category has to do with a time and a place of life. This is highly significant.

The gods that compete for our attention come at us based on the circumstances of our everyday existence. They may have made a few costume changes over the years, but the *categories* are the same.

No Choice but to Choose

We will consider what's behind each of the doors Joshua mentions, but first, it's important to understand the easily missed underlying assumption here, and something I've already assumed in this book: you *will* make a choice.

Joshua doesn't go through the list and say, "Or you could just choose not to worship anything at all." All of us are worshipers. Worship is hardwired in who we are. It's true of every culture and every civilization. Everyone worships. When I was in college I spent a month in Africa with a medical missions team. We went off-road and visited several tribes that had no contact with the outside world. As we entered their communities, the question was not, Are they worshipers? The question was, Who or what do they worship?

The church where I serve is actively involved in planting churches in the northeastern United States. Several times a year I take a trip to the New York City area to visit our new congregations there, and the question is never, Are they worshipers? The question is, Who or what do they worship?

Wherever you go, you see that people have chosen. You will too. It's written into our genetic code. You can go to places where they have old-school idols, rituals, and sacrifices. Or you can go to the most technologically advanced cities, where folks think they're way past what they think of as "religious mumbo jumbo" — though they would probably say something more intelligent sounding than "mumbo jumbo."* But upon closer inspection you find that they are sacrificing a great deal on the altars of power or pleasure or finance. It's really all the same. People are choosing their gods and bringing their offerings. At the end of the day, the real offering is themselves.

Peter Kreeft, a philosopher, puts it this way: "The opposite of theism is not atheism, it's idolatry." In other words everyone is going to worship a god. We were created to be worshipers, as birds were created to fly and rivers were created to flow. It's what we do. The question for you is who or what will be the object of your worship.

Stop and pay attention to the advertising on TV. All of the products are being marketed to the worshiper in us. Companies make their products sound suspiciously like saviors. The not-so-subtle message of nearly every advertisement is: if you're unhappy, bored, or depressed, then buy this product. You will be *saved* from your unhappiness, boredom, and depression. This product is here to redeem you, to deliver you. Talk to your doctor about this medication. Eat at this restaurant. Drive this car. Take this vacation.

They even offer an invitation: Dial this number. Visit this dealer. Order online today. Don't wait; call now. You half expect them to break out into a six-verse version of "Just As I Am." They understand that we are made to worship, and they're making use of that.

Life presents us infinite choices. There are lots of options, with

---

*They would probably say, gobbledygook, hooey, hogwash, or poppycock.

one exception: the option to opt out. There is no box for "none of the above," Joshua says. Pick one.

If we set this scene in a modern context, we would expect a little pushback on this question. Someone would raise his hand and say, "That's all cool and everything, Josh, but we're not really *into* worship. See, we're just not really the religious types."

And there would be lots of nodding heads and "what-he-saids" from the rest of the crowd. "Religion is cool for you and your house, but me and my house just aren't into that."

Here's where we get confused; in our modern thinking, we associate worship with religion.

We think worship has something to do with a lot of robes and rituals and really old music. And if someone doesn't have a drawer in the dresser of their life labeled "organized religion," than they assume that the question of what god they worship doesn't apply to them. You've got drawers labeled "work," "family," "finances," and "hobbies," but not "worship."

The problem, of course, is a misunderstanding of what worship is. When someone answers the question of worship by saying, "I'm not the religious type," he or she is missing the point. If that person is a member of the human race and comes fully equipped with mind and body and emotions, then it follows that the individual is, in fact, a worshiper. It's factory-installed, standard equipment — not a buyer's option.

When you subtract the religious language, worship is the built-in human reflex to put your hope in something or someone and then chase after it. You hold something up and then give your life to pursuing it. If you live in this world, then sooner or later you grow some assumptions concerning what your life is all about, what you should really be going after. And when you begin to align your life with that pursuit, then, whether you realize it or not, you are worshiping.

That's what human beings do, right alongside breathing and

eating and thinking. We identify things we want, both good and bad, and then we make sacrifices to get them. From the time we're born and introduced to milk we are forever pursuing what we think will satisfy our appetites.

The end result, of course, is that our lives begin to take the shape of what we care about most. We each make the choice to worship, and then at some point we discover that the choice makes us. The object of your worship will determine your future and define your life. It's the one choice that all other choices are motivated by.

So Joshua is speaking to all of us when he says, "Choose for yourselves this day whom you will serve." At least, he is saying, make an educated decision on the great goal of your life. Otherwise you will passively flow into some choice by mere osmosis, a little bit of you at a time, until you find yourself inside a temple bowing to a god you never consciously chose.

Four Points on a Compass

Joshua calls the people to choose, and he points to a total of four options. Think of these four options as four points on a compass. Because whatever you choose is going to lead you in a different direction than the others. A lot is at stake because the choice you make will ultimately determine where you end up.

OPTION 1: Gods of Our Fathers (and Mothers)

"The gods your ancestors worshiped
beyond the Euphrates River."
— Joshua 24:14

Long before God spoke to Abraham and told him of the future of his people — a people with a special standing before God — the ancestors of Abraham worshiped the gods of that region. There was a god of the Mesopotamian area for nearly every conceivable purpose. There were three "cosmic" deities, three "astral" ones, and a whole slew of specialized gods and corresponding demons. Dead people came back as spirits to haunt their children. Hills and rocks and mountains were considered to be alive and to have powers.[6]

Abraham came from a society that believed in such gods and held such beliefs. In fact the Bible specifically tells us that Abraham's father was an idol worshiper. Belief in these gods persisted even after the rise of the Hebrew people, through the time of Egyptian slavery, and up to Joshua's era. Now, Joshua wants to know, are they simply going to default to the gods of their forefathers?

It's still a valid question, isn't it? We raise our children in the faith we have — or the lack thereof. We may not do so consciously, but we are constantly erecting idols in our homes and teaching our children about who or what is worthy of our worship.

Think about how this is true for you and the family you were brought up in. Is it possible that the gods that are at war in your life today are the same gods your parents or grandparents worshiped when you were younger?

I recently saw a title on the cover of a magazine that read, "My DNA Made Me Do It." The article was mostly about the fact that you can thank your parents for all your problems. Both your mother and your father contributed to you some twenty-three thousand chromosomes. Some of what you inherited from them is easy to see. You've got your dad's nose or your mom's thighs. But that's not all you picked up from them. We often end up worshiping whatever god they worshiped.

Psychology would affirm the likelihood of this transference. It's called the "law of exposure." The basic premise is that our lives are determined by our thoughts, and our thoughts are determined by what we are exposed to. The law of exposure means that our minds absorb and our lives ultimately reflect whatever we are most frequently exposed to. It shouldn't be surprising then that we have a tendency to worship the gods of our fathers and mothers.

Perhaps nothing was more important to your dad than a successful career. His life revolved around his job. He was willing to sacrifice days off and family vacations to work his way up the ladder. His mood was determined by what kind of day he had at work. His temple was his office, and he worshiped there a good sixty hours a week. And now, is it possible that you worship the gods of success and achievement? Instead of finding your identity and worth in Christ, do you find it in your career?

Maybe your mom cared, or even *obsessed*, about appearances. You remember growing up in a home where everything had to be perfect before company would come over, and she was always updating the house. No one went out in public without every hair perfectly in place. If a neighbor up the street got the new SUV, your mom soon wanted the same model with all the upgrades. She spent a lot of time and money to make sure all of you wore the right clothes from the right stores. Is it possible that you now worship the gods of appearance and perfection? Instead of finding your identity and worth in Christ, do you find it in the clothes you wear, the house you live in, and what other people think of you?

Did your dad worship sports? Sex? Money? Status? Beer?

Did your mom worship shopping? Career? Children? Entertainment?

Don't just skip over those examples. Think about what was held up for you in the home you grew up in. The most natural path in the world is to adopt the gods of our parents.

OPTION 2: Gods of Your Past

"The gods your ancestors worshiped ... in Egypt."
— Joshua 24:14

Joshua specifically mentions the gods from Egypt. These were the gods of the previous generation, gods from the past that never went away.

Like the Mesopotamians, the Egyptians had a diverse and highly developed pantheon of deities. For some reason, they loved mixing and matching human and animal body parts. Horus, god of the delta, had a human body with a falcon head;* Hathor, his partner, had the body of a cow and the head of a woman.†[7] Our kids might recognize these as the Transformers of the ancient world. The Egyptians had their popular gods, but they actually worshiped nearly everything, including the sun, moon, and stars. Smorgasbord worship was their thing.

The Hebrews were Egyptian slaves longer than the United States has been a nation. There was no way they were going to endure that period without absorbing some of the culture around them. Even when Moses led his people out of that land, the gods weren't about to give up without a fight. Old habits, including old worship patterns, die hard. In Ezekiel 20:7, God says "Each of you, get rid of the vile images you have set your eyes on, and do not defile yourselves with the idols of Egypt. I am the LORD your God."

Do you ever find yourself struggling with things from the past that you thought you had left behind a long time ago? When I was in high school, I remember being on my way to pick up a girl for a date. Naturally, I had to walk through her front yard. It was a minefield of doggie-doo. And being nervous about the date, of course, I wasn't watching where my big feet took me.

Her mom answered the door, smiled politely, and invited me in. As I sat on the family sofa next to my date, I noticed a certain unpleasant aroma. I had no clue about its source. I sniffed my date, which, in retrospect, wasn't a good move for a new relationship. I leaned toward her parents — no, they were in the clear. The source of the smell was me — I was ground zero! I looked down at my Doc Martins and realized that I had really stepped in it this time. Quite

---

* Admittedly, that is awesome.

†Which is why you don't know any women named Hathor.

literally. I felt like I was on an episode of *Saved by the Bell* when Zack finally gets a date with Kelly only to have it all go wrong. In horror I looked behind me and realized I had tracked animal excrement through the entryway, across the carpet, and into the parlor. Suddenly I wasn't breathing well.

Here's my point: A lot of people become Christians. They invite Jesus Christ to come into their lives, to take the throne of their heart. Everything is great, but then they catch a strange whiff of something and realize they've brought *stuff* with them. Stuff that is embarrassing. Stuff that is fragrant, and not in a good way. Stuff that should have been destroyed a long time ago but managed to come along for the ride.

It's hard to understand, because they know their sins are forgiven. If they've been thoroughly cleaned, why is this stuff still clinging to them? In many ways, they haven't changed since conversion; they still have the old desires, the old habits. They've invited one Lord into their lives, but they're still paying attention to the old gods. That is the challenge for many of us: the problem isn't that we need to choose to follow Jesus; the problem is that we have tried to follow him without leaving something behind.

In our narrative, Joshua knows that there's a bit of Egypt still clinging to the sandals of his people. Old gods die hard. They hold on, they creep in, they quietly clutch at us. Perhaps when we meet Christ, the old gods fall silent for a while. But they regroup. They wait for their time, and they aim as high as ever. They want to rule our hearts again.

So even if you've chosen the Lord God in the past, the challenge of Joshua is to choose *this day* whom you will serve.

OPTION 3: Gods of Our Culture

"Or the gods of the Amorites,
in whose land you are living."
— Joshua 24:15

Behind the third door were the newcomers to this cosmic clash. These were the people groups of the land the Israelites had just fought so hard to conquer. Whereas the Egyptians had once had the upper hand on God's people, these were the ones God's people had defeated. They were pushed back, overcome, and yet they would continue to be a thorn in Israel's side for the rest of Old Testament times. Their weapon was proximity; these were the gods who hid in plain sight.

The Israelites lived in a place where diversity prevailed, much like in our society. There were many people groups and many different gods. The dominant deity was Baal, whose name meant "owner, master, lord." Sound familiar? Baal had started his career as a god of weather, but expanded into fertility and, from there, to such things as ritual prostitution.

There was also a mother goddess, Ashtoreth. The sacrifices, the temples, the sexual rituals — these things enticed the Israelites, and the prophets of the Old Testament despised them above all other gods.[8] Why? Because these gods had the home field advantage. They were right there.

Two of the most significant factors that consistently determine which gods win the war are time and place. We may be not confronting Baal or Ashtoreth. But we struggle with the gods of our culture every day. We live immersed in what is known as "the spirit of the age," the cultural *zeitgeist*, as it has been called, that is so prevalent it is invisible to us. Fertility rituals and temple prostitution are easy for us to reject, because they don't fit in with our times. For those people, at that time, the worship of these gods was so ingrained that it seemed natural and harmless. Could it be that we have our own idols that are hiding in plain sight, that we don't recognize simply because they're so common?

Paul writes, "Do not conform to the pattern of this world, but be transformed by the renewing of your mind" (Rom. 12:2). "The pattern of this world" is his way of describing the spirit, or the gods, of this age. To go with the flow is to conform to the pattern of this world. J. B. Phillips paraphrased that verse, "Don't let the world around you squeeze you into its own mould."

The Bible advises us to renew our minds by plugging them into the eternal, unchanging truth of the one God.

God Himself

But as for me and my household,
we will serve the LORD.
— Joshua 24:15

This brings us to Joshua's fourth option — the Lord God. The final option, of course, has really been the only option all along. After all, none of the other options are even real. They are nothing more than mirage. They may look promising, but they do nothing to satisfy our thirst.

Before Joshua gives the people these four options, he stacks the deck just a bit by describing all the things God has done for his people over the years. The Lord God had been active and worked powerfully among them — redeeming, protecting, guiding, and providing. So in making a choice, the obvious question for the people to ask of these other gods was, What have they ever done for us?

In making your own choice, I would recommend you ask yourself the same. What enduring value has the god of wealth really bought anyone? Did the gods of pleasure ever once deliver true and lasting happiness? What about the gods of sex? Can they provide a joy that is more than that of a passing moment?

What have these gods done for us? If anything, they have enslaved us. They have robbed us. They have disappointed us.

Tom Brady was asked that question. If you follow football, you'll know that he has been the quarterback for the New England Patriots. He's a superstar, a guy with three Super Bowl rings. He holds pages of passing records, signed a contract for $48 million a couple of years ago, and has dated a succession of supermodels—eventually marrying one of them. By every standard of this world, he has it going on.

That's why we're so surprised to hear his interview on TV's *60 Minutes*. He asked Steve Kroft, the interviewer, "Why do I have three Super Bowl rings and still think there's something greater out there for me? I mean, maybe a lot of people would say, 'Hey man, this is what [it's all about].' I reached my goal, my dream, my life. Me? I think, 'It's got to be more than this.' I mean this isn't —this can't be—all it's cracked up to be."

When Kroft asked him what "the answer" might possibly be, Brady replied, "What's the answer? I wish I knew.... I love playing football, and I love being quarterback for this team. But at the same time, I think there are a lot of other parts about me that I'm trying to find."[9]

Brady is honest and even wise. He knows that a great chunk of the world admires him. He also knows that wealth, fame, power, pleasure, and accomplishment don't provide the ultimate prize in life. He has asked himself, What have those gods done for me? And he has to answer with courageous frankness, "Not enough."

Yet I know people, and you do too, who point to invisible, intangible things when they discuss the meaning of life. They are followers of Jesus Christ, and if you ask them what he has done for them, you'll hear words like *forgiveness, fulfillment, hope, joy,* and *peace*. Psalm 86:8 puts it this way, "Among the gods there is none like you, Lord; no deeds can compare with yours."

Back to Joshua. How do the people respond to his great four-way challenge?

They say exactly the right words. "Then the people answered, 'Far be it from us to forsake the LORD to serve other gods! It was the LORD our God himself who brought us and our parents up out of Egypt, from that land of slavery, and performed those great signs before our eyes. He protected us on our entire journey and among all the nations through which we traveled. And the LORD drove out before us all the nations, including the Amorites, who lived in the land. We too will serve the LORD, because he is our God'" (Josh. 24:16 – 18).

We would expect Joshua to say, "That's what I'm talking about!" Or perhaps something more formal, such as, "You have chosen well!" But oddly, he doesn't let them off the hook so easily. Joshua begins to talk about the *jealousy* of God, the *holiness* of God. He describes the disaster that will come upon them if they don't live up to the words they're speaking.

Joshua, you see, is an old man. He has watched these people all his life. He knows how fickle their hearts are, how quickly their attention wanders. He knows how easily they say the right things, only to turn around and make the wrong choices. It's so simple to produce the right platitudes on cue, as they have done here, but it's so hard to keep living the truth. And so a warning is issued.

This story has a cautionary ending. It comes only two Bible chapters after the one we've been reading. "Joshua son of Nun, the servant of the LORD, died at the age of a hundred and ten. And they buried him in the land of his inheritance, at Timnath Heres in the hill country of Ephraim, north of Mount Gaash. After that whole generation had been gathered to their ancestors, another generation grew up who knew neither the LORD nor what he had done for Israel" (Judg. 2:8 – 10).

We've said it more than once: the gods never surrender. They may lose a generation, but even then, they say, "We'll get the next one." They may lose you for a day, but they'll be back tomorrow.

Idol ID

We are all wired for worship, and our choices are a strong indication of what gods we are worshiping.

What I choose to do for a living.

How I choose to manage my money.

What I choose to watch on TV.

The people I choose to have as friends.

The websites I choose to visit.

The clothes I choose to wear.

The way I choose to spend my day off.

The food I choose to eat.

What I choose to think about.

All of these choices reveal my god of choice.

So instead of me asking you about what gods you are worshiping, let me ask you about what choices you are making. Stop for a moment and consider your options, and then choose carefully.

How close are your choices to those of your parents?

Consider those things you will do or decide this week. How many of them reflect the thinking and values of your parents? Do you vote the same political party? Do you pursue the same goals? Do you sacrifice for the same things? Is it possible that you are worshiping the same "gods beyond the river" that your parents worshiped?

What gods and goals have you inherited without really realizing it?

If you have chosen to worship the Lord God, how much of that is your parents' decision, and how much is your own?

What gods would you identify as the "gods of culture"?

Perhaps this is the question that requires the most demanding reflection, because these gods are often such a part of our daily lives that we don't recognize them. But take a moment and look at the world around you through the lens of idolatry. Can you recognize the true American idols?

Think of two or three movies or television shows you've watched recently. Bring to mind a few of the popular songs today. What is held up and pursued? What are the gods that our culture glorifies and honors?

How has following Christ impacted your choices?

If you are a follower of Jesus, how do your choices differ from those of your parents, your past, and your culture?

Do you approach money and possessions differently than your parents?

Have your priorities or pursuits changed since you started following Jesus? Are you still living for the same things?

What choices have you made that go against our cultural ideals because you are a follower of Jesus? Is there anything about your sex life or entertainment choices that sets you apart from the world?

**What past priorities and pursuits continue
to influence you?**
Is there something or someone from your past that took
the place of the Lord God in your life? A god that you were
living for? What stuff is on the bottom of your shoes? What
gods from your past continue to war for the throne of your
heart? What do you need to leave behind in order to follow
Jesus more completely?

part 2

the temple
of pleasure

Have you ever thought about the place of pleasure in modern life? I'm talking about the plain old pursuit of fun in all its forms.

There have always been games, stories, jokes, and songs, but today pleasure is something close to the whole theme of daily living. We even expect our daily work to be pleasurable, much more than our ancestors did. In a society based on agriculture, nobody said, "Know what? Plowing and tending cattle aren't enough fun for me."

But these days if it isn't fun, if it isn't pleasurable, we don't want to do it. We have more leisure time and more money to spend on it. And how much do we spend? Well, it depends on what kinds of things you specify as part of the "pleasure industry."

We know this much: people spend trillions of dollars each year trying to make themselves happy, whether it's with food, with various forms of entertainment media, with travel, with drugs or drink, or with one of the countless other items that promise to turn your frown upside down.

In a postindustrial society, our survival needs are met. We sold the farm after all, and we've gathered in cities where we have food, shelter, plenty of water, and a surplus of time.

I know what you're thinking, No one has a surplus of time; we are busier than ever. Fair enough, but what are we busy doing? Quite often, the answer is chasing pleasure.

When we experience pleasure, there's a part of us that thinks, Yes! This is what I was made for. Even if you haven't experienced much pleasure in your life, you've experienced enough to know that you want more. Thus begins the quest for the elusive narcotic of pleasure.

And so the gods of pleasure whisper, "Wouldn't you like to scratch that itch? Wouldn't you like to satisfy that appetite? Wouldn't you like to experience that feeling? Wouldn't you like to get that high? I have what you are looking for right here."

And so we walk into the temple of pleasure. And there we see the gods of food, sex, and entertainment. There are others, to be sure, but these are the ones we most often find ourselves bowing down to. And when we begin to worship pleasure, the end result is always *pain*.

Just to be clear, I want to say right from the start that food, sex, and entertainment are not sinful or evil in and of themselves. In fact these things all have the potential to be good gifts from God that draw our hearts to him all the more. But inside the temple of pleasure, gifts are turned into gods.

Remember Joshua's impassioned speech to the people challenging them to choose which god they would serve? The people chose the Lord God, and they were told to throw away the gods of the Egyptians.

But instead of destroying the old gods, they put them in storage. Several hundred years pass, and the nation of Israel splits into two. There is the northern kingdom and the southern kingdom. The first king of the northern kingdom is Jeroboam, and he doesn't want his people going to Jerusalem in the southern kingdom to worship God. Besides making his own gods, he also decides to grab the keys to the storage unit and pull out the gods of the Egyptians for the people to worship.

The worship of these idols continues as the kings come and go. Then a man named Ahab, son of Omri, ascends to the throne of

Israel. And we read that he "did more evil in the eyes of the LORD than any of those before him" (1 Kings 16:30).

This king marries a woman named Jezebel whose name is still in your dictionary as another word for "an immoral or manipulative woman." She sets up an altar and a temple for the god of Baal in Samaria.

Jezebel has many prophets of the true God killed — and God, as we have seen, is jealous. He reaches the point where he has had enough of the people's unfaithfulness and he sends his prophet Elijah to Ahab. Elijah says to the king, "As the LORD, the God of Israel, lives, whom I serve, there will be neither dew nor rain in the next few years except at my word" (1 Kings 17:1).

Save your bottled water — a drought is coming.

Please understand: weather is Baal's thing. His number one talent, supposedly, is taking care of meteorological issues. This is why the genuine God withholds rain; it's the most obvious way to get the attention of unfaithful people. It's obviously their biggest item of interest.

God withholds his blessing in the very areas in which we lift up false gods.

For example, has anyone noticed any significant economic problems in our money-obsessed culture lately?

How about problems with food — obesity, junk food issues, nutritional issues?

What about sex? Anybody see any sexual dysfunction in our culture?

How about the entertainment industry? Isn't it interesting that one of the most common complaints of our entertainment-saturated society is boredom?

We shouldn't be surprised. After all, why would the Lord God bless us in the area that represents his greatest competition? So ask yourself: Is it possible that you're seeing a financial drought, a sexual satisfaction drought, or some other kind of challenge, because you want it so bad that it has become a god?

I'm not saying that's always the case, but you shouldn't expect God to help you down the path of chasing after an idol. He's not going to bless the one area of your life that is robbing him of his place on the throne of your heart. Why would God bless his primary competition?

Like Joshua, Elijah demands that the people stand, define the choice for what it is, and name their path: "Elijah went before the people and said, 'How long will you waver between two opinions? If the LORD is God, follow him; but if Baal is God, follow him.' But the people said nothing" (1 Kings 18:21).

It's a passage that is strikingly similar to Joshua 24, with the exception that the people are silent this time. And why? Could it be that, in the midst of a drought, they didn't want to make that choice? That they wanted to have it both ways?

They wanted to be followers of the Lord God, but they also wanted to be followers of Baal — after all, there was a drought in the land and they needed to cover all the bases. They wanted both, and so they said nothing.

As we look at these gods of pleasure in the next section of this book I think you will find that the same is true of us. When forced to choose between the Lord God and the god of pleasure, we say nothing. Why? Because we want both.

chapter 5

the god
of food

Paul Jones had a doting mother, and he was certainly a doting son. Together, the two of them constituted a self-contained world, population two.

Almost from the beginning, they had depended upon each other. Paul's father was an over-the-road truck driver, usually a thousand miles away on some interstate adventure. He came home with tired and distant eyes. His road trips stretched ever longer, until the day he didn't come home at all.

Paul was eight or nine by then. He had no brothers and sisters, and few friends his age. His best friend was his mother. Like him, she had been an only child. So the two of them played together, pretended together, were inseparable.

When Paul was sick, a frequent occurrence, his mother fussed over him desperately. Paul began to be conscious of the pressure he felt to stay well, to do well, to make her happy; after all, he was all she had, so he had to be worth her while.

His diary contained lots of entries about restaurants. That was their thing, Paul and his mom. He recorded the venues, the dishes, the quality of the cooking, and any plans for the next dining adventure.

When Paul was in sixth grade, he would climb onto the school bus and avoid looking at the driver. A man sitting behind the wheel of a large vehicle made him think of his father. He avoided the eyes of most of the kids too. They were snickering, making fun of his size. Paul was already in the throes of childhood obesity.

At the end of the day, he had to ride the bus again, climb off at his stop, and be heckled all the way home. Behind the locked door, he would find comfort in whatever snack his mother had prepared. There was always a snack, and it served as his refuge from the traumas of adolescence for an overweight boy. Mom just wanted him to be happy, and she had her own issues with overeating, so how could she help someone else?

Church? Well, it never entered the equation. Paul's mother had little use for God. She had seen more than her share of hypocrisy in churches, and there had come a moment many years ago when she had said, "As soon as I'm old enough to make my own decisions, I'm out of here. I'll never walk inside a church again."

During high school, Paul's life began to improve. A ninth-grade teacher took a genuine interest in him and made him feel important, as if his weight didn't disqualify him from having a good life. Maybe it was possible for him to have dignity and significance as a human being. The teacher made a difference. Paul reached inside and found some strength to rally and made a place for himself at school.

But he still had to do something with his pain; it never really went away. He discovered he could be a chameleon, capable of blending into any background. Teachers and parents praised him for doing such deeds as joining civic groups, visiting nursing homes, and reading to patients there. Meanwhile, he was also drinking, partying, and cutting classes.

He tried to fit everywhere, only to find that he didn't fit anywhere.

Paul's mother could see the contradictions of his life, but she couldn't reach him. The more she pushed to find a way in, the more he pushed her out. He had foreseen that cutting the apron strings, whenever it happened, would be a terrible moment, and it was. She wasn't going down without a fight. It ended with shouting, bitter words, and Paul — having been kicked out — moving five hundred miles away.

It wasn't long before he found himself engaged to be married, living in Alabama with the family of his fiancée. These people accepted him. It was the first time he had been around people who took their faith seriously, and they were clearly different. Could it be that he had found his place here in the Bible Belt, of all places? His new friends calmed his raging spirit as they led him to Christ, and he began studying the Bible with an insatiable hunger.

The physical hunger, however, wasn't going away so easily. The gods of food who had provided him comfort, security, and confidence bided their time. Very soon — even with Christ in the picture — those gods would counterattack.

Comfort Food

There's an animated feature film called *Over the Hedge*. It's about a group of animals from the woods who decide to move to the suburbs. RJ the raccoon has made a discovery: human beings, who dwell there, are bottomless pits of food. If the animals just hang around the hedges, there will always be something to eat. "We eat to live," RJ says. "These guys live to eat."

Then he offers to show the other animals what he's talking about. They peek in on a human family, and RJ explains that the human mouth is called a "pie hole." The person himself is a "couch potato." Telephones are devices for summoning food — one is used and, sure enough, a pizza delivery boy turns up.

RJ says, "Humans bring the food, take the food, ship the food, and drive the food." He points to passing trucks with pictures of food on them. It seems that everything people do involves food.

"That is the altar where they worship food," says RJ as the family prays around the dinner table. He points to a treadmill:

"That gets rid of guilt so they can eat more food. Food! Food! Food!"

This may be a new way of thinking about food, but before you write it off and head to the fridge, think for a moment of the role it plays in our lives. For example, consider this number: $110 billion. That's one estimate of the amount that Americans will spend consuming fast food alone this year. It's more than the amount that will be spent on movies, books, magazines, newspapers, videos, and recorded music *combined*.

According to the American Center for Disease Control, 68 percent of Americans are overweight, and one-third of Americans are obese. It would be hard to argue that the god of food is less than a central power in this country.

But the scales don't tell the whole story, do they? You could happen to have a strong metabolism and look very fit, but food could still be a god for you. I have a great friend who annoys me to no end because he can eat whatever he wants and never gain any weight. He's always whining about how he needs to gain more weight.

Food can also be a god when you are consumed with diet and exercise. You could build your life around organic health foods, and you'd still be building your life around a false god, if a more physically healthy one. But it's a god that can demand incredible sacrifice of time and money. It's a god that specializes in vanity — an obsession with outward appearance. He gets you to worship your own image.

In the Scriptures, food is always a gift from heaven. God showed Adam and Eve the great bounty of good things he had prepared for them to eat. Clearly he wanted eating to be a joyful thing, not simply a matter of bodily fuel maintenance. He created a vast spectrum of foods and flavors, then gave us ten thousand taste buds to provide that flavor in high-definition tasting.

We are told, "Go, eat your food with gladness" (Eccl. 9:7). God could have provided some simple root for us to chew on that would supply all our nutritional needs. But he is lavish in his gifts, insistent that we get the full range of joy in the things he has given us — including food.

Eating is good. The problem is that every gift God gives us can be twisted into a lure to pull us away from him.

Think about how the god of food works. Imagine walking into one of his favorite temples, the Cheesecake Factory. Ever been there? It's one of my favorites too. As the hostess shows you to your table, you steal glances at what others are having. This decision will be tough!

At the table, she hands you a menu that is so thick it has to be divided into chapters. You don't even know where to begin in such a taste bud fantasyland.

What's really going on here? I certainly don't go to good restaurants simply for bodily sustenance. I could chew on some root; it would probably be a healthy choice. No, it's all about *satisfaction*. We want to throw a big, raucous party between the tongue and the tonsil. And for just a few minutes, all is right with the world. It's a little piece of heaven.

Little piece of heaven? That phrase probably didn't strike you as out of place in the above scenario. Notice how often we invoke heaven or spirituality when we talk about the pleasure of eating: "This cake is heavenly"; "this pie is to die for"; "soul food"; "angel food cake"; "I thought I'd died and gone to heaven"; "death by chocolate"; "nectar of the gods."

I feel like I need to make something clear again, and you will probably get tired of this reminder, but it's an important one. There is nothing wrong with eating at the Cheesecake Factory. It's not idolatry to enjoy a great meal. The problem comes when we start to look to food to do for us what the Lord God alone should do.

Why would we do that? Well, maybe the day brought its share of disappointments. Maybe you didn't snare the promotion you were looking for; maybe you had to endure another snarky email from the boss; maybe the work itself has become drudgery for you. Maybe it's family issues, and the thought of going home makes work seem like a day at the beach.

Instead of turning to God, how often do we try to treat a troubled soul as if it were a growling stomach? Have you found that nothing is better at the end of a long day than the Blue Bell Pralines and Cream ice cream? Just a random example.

When the going gets tough, the tough get chewing. It provides a quick and obvious shot of comfort. Big, dripping hamburgers on billboards; pizza commercials on the radio; fast food emporiums with drive-through windows, all along the road on your way home from work—all of these are promising to make you feel better. We even call it "comfort food."

HUNGER PAINS

The average American consumes two to three pounds of sugar per week. A little over a century ago, when heart disease and cancer were not nearly so common, the average person consumed five pounds *per year.*

During the last two decades, we've increased our sugar intake by a factor of five. We're looking for that quick boost that sugar gives, but sugar can also trigger a boost in stress hormones that may remain for five hours. Over that period, your body is coping with excess insulin and a depletion of healthy glucose levels.

So that carton of ice cream is the last place you should turn in a moment of anxiety. Call it *dis*comfort food.[*]

[*] Teresa Aubele, "Why a Sugar High Leads to a Brain Low," *Psychology Today*, October 18, 2011, www.psychologytoday.com/blog/prime-your-gray-cells/201110/why-sugar-high-leads-brain-low (accessed September 28, 2012).

But think about this: *Comforter* is what God calls himself. He is the God of all comfort and he is ready to talk with you about your day. The Prince of Peace waits to give you his gifts and strengthen you. He wants to be your satisfaction. Frank Ferrell has written, "A very large part of mankind's ills and of the world's misery is due to the rampant practice of trying to feed the soul with the body's food."

Counterfeit Lover

Paul Jones had found Jesus, but his life continued a downward spiral. His marriage ended rather abruptly in divorce, and when he lost his wife, that left him alone in Alabama with no friends. He was lonelier and more miserable than ever.

He needed comfort and salvation and there seemed to be nowhere to turn but the refrigerator. He was out of control in his eating habits now, and he hardly noticed that each season, he had to buy all new clothes. Size 44 was the new size 42, and next season it would be 46. It was all fairly gradual, and he didn't think much about it. Overeating had always been a part of his life, and he knew no other lifestyle. But it now grew until it had crowded out nearly everything else.

He went to churches and discovered that they had food issues too. Nearly every activity involved some food angle — covered dish dinners, ice cream socials, Wednesday night Bible studies over dinner. Not that Paul complained; it fit right into who he was.

By 1990, Paul felt a strong call to serve God full time in ministry. So he moved to Louisville and began attending seminary. There he met his second wife, Renée, and he knew God had done something wonderful for him — a second chance at having a life partner. He did his best to ignore the fact that he had a twelve-thousand-calorie-per-day monkey on his back. His weight was 435 pounds. Ten medications were required for his daily life as he found himself dealing with diabetes, high cholesterol and blood pressure, and sleep apnea.

The gods of food were closing in, demanding more and more from him.

He was eating just to eat and deriving much less pleasure from it. Often he had to immediately regurgitate the pizza or multiple hamburgers because even his massive frame couldn't handle the quantities his addiction demanded. Renée, too, was gaining weight, so the two of them, even as intentional followers of Christ, quietly made their sacrifices to the insistent, sacrifice-craving god of food.

Eventually his body revolted. His heart raced; he had attacks of panic and anxiety; he couldn't breathe; he trembled. It felt to him as if this was it, that he was dying.

The doctors had no answers. Paul needed help, needed it desperately, and he turned to the counselors at the church he and Renée were attending. A pastoral counselor gave him an appointment, and Paul found himself sitting on the man's floor — as was often the case because there were no chairs with the space to accommodate him.

He was crying, telling his story, totally lost and in despair. He was in a dark place, desperate for someone to turn on a light.

A Different Kind of Bread

The gospel of John records a moment in the ministry of Jesus where we see food become his competition. In John 6, the people are forced to choose between food to satisfy their hunger or Jesus to satisfy their souls.

Jesus looked upon a massive crowd; the count is given as five thousand, but that would only account for the men present. There may have been as many as fifteen thousand there.

They had to eat. You're probably familiar with what happened:

he fed them miraculously with just five barley loaves and a couple of fish. John 6 tells us they ate until everyone was filled.

They saw it as dining out, but he saw it as an object lesson. He wanted these people to hunger and thirst for righteousness. He wanted them to discover the truth of what he taught in the Sermon on the Mount when he said, "Is not life more than food?" (Matt. 6:25). Jesus had gone into the wilderness for forty days and nights at the beginning of his ministry, to fast so that food wouldn't get in the way of hearing from God.

How could he get people to see what he saw — to accept physical food as they needed it, then focus on the spiritual food that provided eternal nourishment? He wanted them to have the kind of passion for filling the soul that they did for filling the stomach.

After everyone had eaten their fill, Jesus sneaked away during the night to the other side of the lake. He wanted to put some distance between himself and the clamoring masses.

Back on the other shore, the crowds woke up the next morning and saw that Jesus and his disciples had shoved off. So they followed along after him. After all, yesterday's feast was digested and gone. What was on the menu for today? Surely Jesus was open for breakfast.

They caught up with him on the far side of the lake, and here's what he told them: "Do not work for food that spoils, but for food that endures to eternal life, which the Son of Man will give you" (John 6:27).

Jesus told them all they had to do was to believe in him.

You have to love their reply to that. They suggested he give them a sign so they could believe, and that a really nice one would be, oh, let's say, some of that nice, fresh bread from heaven that God had sent to Moses and his people. They helpfully quoted the Scriptures for him: "Our ancestors ate the manna in the wilderness; as it is written: 'He gave them bread from heaven to eat'" (John 6:31).

It doesn't record whether someone added, "Just sayin'."

The crowd definitely had bread on the brain, but can you imagine asking Jesus to legitimize himself with a sign, when he had just fed a crowd of probably fifteen thousand on a few loaves and fishes?

Jesus finally replied, "I am the bread of life. Whoever comes to me will never go hungry, and whoever believes in me will never be thirsty" (John 6:35).

Jesus tells this crowd that, though they can't see it, *he* is the bread they are looking for. They come wanting something to eat, and Jesus offers them himself.

But here's the question: Is he enough?

Our answer comes in verse 66. We're told that from this moment on, many people stopped following Jesus. They chose what god they would worship, and it clearly wasn't Jesus.

What about you? Will you continue to follow even without a meal ticket? What's more important to you: food for your stomach or food for your soul?

Paul's Three Journeys

Paul Jones began walking his third road after that broken-down visit to the church counselor. The first journey had been that of growing up with unhealthy self-esteem and a dysfunctional relationship with food. The second journey started on the day he began walking with Christ, and he was sure it was the ultimate path to follow. He was right, but something was still wrong.

He had brought along an idol, the god of food. And there was room for only one Lord in his life. Now, as he sat on the counselor's floor, it was all becoming clear to him.

He understood why God had seemed silent. He was waiting for Paul to become totally dependent upon him. It had taken thirteen frustrating years for Paul to hit bottom. During that time, he was always the man with the plan — and all those plans crashed. Finally he was ready to listen to a plan that originated with God.

Soon he was back home, looking at his bathroom mirror and weeping as he prayed: "God, I don't know what to do anymore. I quit. I just quit."

And in the quietness of his spirit, he heard God's answer: "I've been waiting so long to hear those words from you, Paul. Stop trying so hard. Stop planning, and let me be your guide. Let me lay it all out for you. All you have to do is let go."

From that moment, things were different — *really* different, this time. God began to rebuild a broken man from the inside out. It seemed to Paul that the scales had fallen from his eyes, and now he could understand his childhood. He knew why he had done the things he had done: it was the slow-motion suicide of worshiping the god of the stomach.

He knew there were unhealed wounds involving his father, involving the broken relationship with his mother, and so many other hurts. There still would be much to deal with, but he could do it; Christ would be with him. Christ had a plan for him after all. Now he was ready to give up the plastic ecstasy of eating for a joy that was real.

Every now and then, old habits set in during weak moments. But Paul was startled to discover that if he tried to abuse food, it no longer had any real taste.

He wasn't thinking much about losing weight, really — just about getting through another day, learning to be this new person. It was surrendering his soul, not going on a diet. Even so, he and Renée began to notice that his clothes were getting baggy.

He would go out and take long walks, especially in the rain — he *loved* walking in the rain — but it wasn't about exercise; it was so easy to talk with God on those excursions. He got up and walked in the morning, he walked when he had any kind of down time, and then, occasionally, there would be a shock — he'd realize he had actually forgotten a meal.

Who is this person? he thought. Only now did he fully realize what food had been to him.

And soon he was actually running — a mile, then eventually a mini-marathon, and then an honest-to-goodness twenty-six-mile *marathon*. Just like the serious runners.

And in time, Paul Jones, who had once weighed over four hundred pounds, who had relied on ten different medications just to get through the day — that same Paul Jones finally found a deeper purpose for his life. He became, of all things, a fitness instructor at his church. He knew his life was a miracle.

He thanks God for this true pleasure, and thinks about what Jesus said: "Blessed are those who hunger and thirst for righteousness, for they will be filled" (Matt. 5:6).

This journey for Paul Jones had not been comfortable. "But God is not interested in my comfort," he said. "He's interested in my healing."

For that to take place, an idol had to be smashed, the god of pleasure called food. *Pleasure?* What an irony that was — Paul Jones never knew true pleasure until physical food was replaced with the bread of life.

God cannot and will not give us a sense of lasting pleasure apart from him, because it violates his purpose and our design. Psalm 34:8 reads, "Taste and see that the LORD is good."

Chew on that for a while the next time the god of food calls out to you.

Idol ID

Do you eat more for pleasure or for nourishment?

Take a look at your eating habits and discern why you eat what you eat. Is it mostly because of pleasure or nourishment? Again, there is nothing wrong in finding pleasure from a gift that the Lord God has given us; but when we pursue pleasure for its own sake it has a way of expanding beyond its borders.

In 1 Corinthians 10:31, Paul explains that instead of being an object of worship, what we eat can be an act of worship. He wrote, "So whether you eat or drink or whatever you do, do it all for the glory of God."

When and why do you overindulge?

How often do you buy into the concept of "comfort food"? Do you use it as a salve for daily wounds?

When life goes wrong, our first impulse frequently is to turn to food. It's easy, it's readily available, and the sense of taste is a powerful distraction.

Consider the times of day that you do this. Is it on the way home from work when you're trying to deal with life? Is it after everyone else is in bed and you decide you should reward yourself?

Would you be willing to try a fast?

One of the easiest ways to gauge the power that the god of food has over you is to go on a fast. How hard would it be for you to fast for three days, one day, or even just from certain foods?

Don't do it as a test of discipline or as a way to fit into your skinny jeans in the closet. Do it for the expressed purpose of spending time with God. Pray that you will have greater hunger for him than for the food of this world.

CHOOSING JESUS:

Jesus My Portion

*Idols are defeated not by being removed
but by being replaced.*

The god of food promised us a feast, but we came up empty. He invited us to consume until it consumed our lives. We tasted everything until nothing had taste anymore.

And so finally we came to Jesus. We discovered that he offers the one true feast. He fills our every need. Every hunger ultimately leads back to him.

David wrote, "LORD, you alone are my portion and my cup; you make my lot secure" (Ps. 16:5).

Jesus frees us from an abusive, dysfunctional relationship with food because he is our portion and in him we discover what we were searching for all along. If we seek our joy and meaning in food, then the source of our joy always disappears and always must be found again — a consumable god. It is different with Jesus.

Nothing tastes better than the joy and satisfaction of knowing Christ. Nothing nourishes the soul as he does. Nothing feeds and strengthens and renews us like the time we spend with him each day.

He bids us to take and eat. He bids us to come to the well where he offers living water, so that we never thirst again.

Think of a time when you've come in from the hot

sun, drenched with sweat and with a parched throat, and downed a cool glass of ice water. Did anything ever taste better?

Such a moment is no more than a vague hint of what it feels like to be spiritually starving and to be given the bread of life, to have a thirsty soul and to drink deep from his living water.

Ironically, it is only when we find our meaning in Christ, when he takes the throne of our lives, that earthly food recovers its taste, its delight. In its right place food is a great gift from God.

the god
of sex

Sex is good.

I just want to be real clear about that early on.

In fact, sex is a gift from God himself. But isn't it amazing how some of the richest and most beautiful gifts from God are often the same gifts that are twisted into hideous and destructive idols?

Sex was God's idea. He designed it to intimately connect us to a spouse. Sex, done God's way, can create a supernatural bond between us. At the creation of humanity, it was arranged by God that "a man leaves his father and mother and is joined to his wife, and the two are united into one" (Gen. 2:24 NLT).

This is a *spiritual* union that is captured and reflected in the physical act of making love. One of the Hebrew words for sex, translated literally, is "a mingling of the souls," and that captures it perfectly — a beautiful gift from God.

It brings pleasure and intimacy, and of course it produces children, in accordance with God's plan. He could have made reproduction simple, mechanical, a joyless act of natural instinct. He could have created sex to feel the same way it feels when your hair grows. But he chose to make it pleasurable.

Just as we've seen with food, God designed sex in such a way that it doesn't just accomplish a purpose; it also brings pleasure. He is a father who likes to give his children good things.

All his gifts point us back to him. Or at least that's how it should work. The gift should cause us to love and worship the giver more deeply. But all too easily God's gifts to us end up being his greatest competition.

Imagine for a moment that you're a parent out shopping for a present to give your child. You've heard him talking, in tones of awe, about the latest gaming console. You see it at the store, and the thought of the smile on his face puts a smile on yours. It's not inexpensive; in fact it's somewhat of a sacrifice. But you want the best for your child.

When you get home and present the gift, your child offers a joyful shout, a tight hug, and a dozen frenzied thank-yous. It was worth every penny for this moment. You stop by his room a couple of times and watch him setting it up and playing it with utter concentration. You ask him a question about the game, and he says, "Wait — can't talk," and then seems to forget you're there.

Later you ask him to go out to dinner with the family, but he begs off, wanting only to stay and play with his new game. Later on he starts to tell you about the add-ons and games his friends have, arguing that their version is much better than his. Not only do you not see him as much as before, but he seems less content and happy than before you bought this console. How could a nice gift go so wrong?

It happened because the gift became more important than the giver. The beauty was not meant to be so much in the thing itself, but the love that brought it about.

This is what happens when God has to compete with his own blessings. Sex is beautiful until it loses its spiritual context. Food and other forms of pleasure are wonderful until they become ends in themselves. They become gods, and the gods become tyrants, and the tyrants become slave masters.

A Fairy Tale Gone Wrong

There's an old story about a prince and a princess. But this one is unlike any found in storybooks, and Disney is unlikely to create an animated feature film out of it. It's told in the Bible in 2 Samuel 13, and it's a true story.

David, the king of Israel, in keeping with the custom of his time, had various wives and various children by them. It's worth noting that, far from approving or even condoning polygamy, the Old Testament provides one example after another of why it doesn't work.

The main characters are Amnon, one of David's sons, a prince of Israel, and Tamar, David's daughter by a different wife, a princess of Israel.

Amnon and Tamar, then, are half siblings. And the Bible says this: "Amnon became so obsessed with his sister Tamar that he made himself ill" (2 Sam. 13:2).

Obsession is an idolatry word. Amnon was constantly thinking about and focusing on one image in his mind, one possibility. He allowed this fantasy to fill his heart until he made himself sick with lust.

Amnon had a friend and advisor who wanted to know why the prince was looking so rough. Amnon explained that he couldn't get the thought of being with Tamar out of his mind. The advisor then gave him the following advice: "Okay, Amnon, here's what you do. Call in sick to the palace today. Then your dad, the king, will be worried, and he'll come to check up on you. You tell him that it would really help your recovery if your sister Tamar were to come in and bake you some of her homemade bread.

"Then, of course, when she comes in, you'll tell her you just love to watch her cooking. Then, my man, I think you can take it from there, right?"

Amnon went with it. When his half sister came in to cook for him, he said to her, "Tell the servants we won't be needing them this evening." Then he instructed her to come to the bedroom and feed him the bread.

What happened next is heartbreaking. He pushed the food aside and declared what was on his mind. She resisted. She pled for him to think about what he was doing, to think about the disgrace it would inflict upon her, to think about his own reputation.

The Bible says, "But he refused to listen to her, and since he was stronger than she, he raped her" (2 Sam. 13:14).

Tamar did what the people of her time did to demonstrate great mourning and suffering. She put ashes on her head and tore the beautiful robe she was wearing. These actions also symbolized her loss of virginity. She left weeping and broken.

Amnon's sexual sin brought incredible destruction and devastation, not just upon his family but on the entire nation. The disruption to a royal family means disruption to a countryside. Everything spiraled wildly out of control, but where did it all begin? It began with idolatry. He chose to worship the god of sexual pleasure. He spent countless hours lusting after Tamar until it became his obsession.

I know what you're thinking: What in the world does this story have to do with me? We would never go down such a path or commit such a heinous act. But that's exactly the kind of thing I'm sure Amnon said to himself before this happened. The god of sex specializes in taking you further than you ever intended to go.

So let me ask you, has the pursuit of sexual pleasure become an obsession? Is it the subject of your last thought at night and your first in the morning? Do you daydream about it at work, spend money on it, risk your career and marriage for it? Is it what you fight about most in your marriage?

Do you feel the presence of God fading into the deepening mist of a cloud of shame?

The Pleasure Paradox

When something good becomes a god, the pleasure it brings dies in the process. Pleasure has this unique trait: the more intensely you chase it, the less likely you are to catch it.

Philosophers call this the "hedonistic paradox." The idea is that pleasure, pursued for its own sake, evaporates before our eyes. The Bible records how Amnon responded when he finally gave in to his lust. It didn't satisfy him the way he thought it would. It was the opposite. The incident lasted just a matter of moments, and when it was over he looked upon her with contempt, even with "intense hatred."

According to the Scriptures, "He hated her more than he had loved her" (2 Sam. 13:15).

What a strange verse. "He hated her more than he had loved her." What does that mean? She didn't do anything to him. It doesn't make any sense.

But I'm guessing some of you have an idea about what's going on here. The god of sexual pleasure promises you incredible satisfaction. As you read magazines and surf websites, as you keep going a little bit farther with your boyfriend or girlfriend, you obsess over what it would be like to push the envelope, to go ahead and give in to your desires, to grab that moment of ecstasy.

But what happens? The god delivers the opposite of what is promised.

Instead of satisfaction, you experience emptiness and an almost immediate hunger for something more. Instead of closeness and intimacy, you experience a strange sense of something that feels like loneliness.

You think that the steak will match the sizzle, that it all will pay off, that you will feel complete. Instead, you can't shake the impression that you've given away some part of yourself that you can't get back.

When the gift replaces the giver as the object of our worship, something surprising happens. When we begin to worship this god of pleasure instead of the God who gave it to us, we discover that the pleasure is lost. We discover the devastating paradox that when we pursue pleasure as a god, pleasure disappears.

The Morning After

Let's go back to our story of Elijah. The drought had brought devastation to the land. Elijah goes to King Ahab and sets up what amounts to a cage match between the Lord God and the gods of Baal and Asherah. People from all over Israel gather on Mount Carmel to watch the "battle of the gods." On one side is Elijah, rep-

---

COUNTING THE COST

What's the long-term effect of viewing pornography? Professors Dolf Zillman of Indiana University and Jennings Bryant of the University of Houston tell us their findings:

- *Decreased satisfaction with one's sexual partner.* Men find their wives or partners less attractive and sex less satisfying. They're also less satisfied with their partners' sexual drive and sexual curiosity.

- *A decrease in how much one values faithfulness.* Sex outside marriage begins to seem less forbidden, more of a real option.

- *A major increase in the importance of sex without attachment.* Sex becomes a physical act, rather than an intimate connection. It isolates people.[*]

---

[*] D. Zillman and J. Bryant, "Pornography's Impact on Sexual Satisfaction," *Journal of Applied Social Psychology* 18, no. 5 (1988): 438–53; and D. Zillman and J. Bryant, "Effects of Prolonged Consumption of Pornography on Family Values," *Journal of Family Issues* 9, no. 4 (December 1988): 518–44.

resenting the Lord; on the other side are 850 prophets representing the false gods. Elijah says to the 850 prophets:

> "Choose one of the bulls and prepare it first, since there are so many of you. Call on the name of your god, but do not light the fire." So they took the bull given them and prepared it. Then they called on the name of Baal from morning till noon. "Baal, answer us!" they shouted. But there was no response; no one answered. And they danced around the altar they had made.
> At noon Elijah began to taunt them. "Shout louder!" he said. "Surely he is a god! Perhaps he is deep in thought, or busy* or traveling. Maybe he is sleeping and must be awakened." So they shouted louder and slashed themselves with swords and spears, as was their custom, until their blood flowed.
>
> —1 Kings 18:25–28

What a sight it must have been. These prophets are cutting and slashing themselves, desperate to get the attention of their god. We shake our heads at the ridiculousness of such behavior. They worship their false god with greater and greater intensity, thinking that if they just give a little more, then their god will respond. This all seems so primitive. How can it be relevant to us today?

But have we not bled upon the altar of sexual pleasure?

Some have sacrificed their finances. More money is spent on pornography in this country every year than on rock music, country music, jazz, and classical music put together. More money is spent on pornography than pro baseball, basketball, and football combined. Last year it grossed more than ABC, NBC, CBS, and FOX combined. It's an industry worth more than ten billion dollars annually.

But it's not just our money we've sacrificed to this god. Many

---

*Literal translation for *busy* is "Maybe he's relieving himself." Seriously.

have sacrificed their marriages, their children, and their careers on its altar.

As a pastor I have had many men, and increasingly women, come to me and talk about their addiction to pornography. I look into their eyes and see what this cruel god has required of them. I see how they have slashed at themselves until they are weak and miserable.

I've talked to men and women who are in bondage to extramarital affairs. It started with flattering remarks from a coworker — a little smile here, a suggestion there, a friend request is accepted. Now their marriages are destroyed.

I've had high school students write to me, telling me how online images that used to disgust them are now the very images they require for arousal. They don't know who they are becoming or where it will all lead. They have so much despair, yet they're only in their teens.

Another woman has led a life of secret sin for years, and she hooks up through Facebook and Craigslist. She can't find the exit door.

"It's just looking at pictures," we say. "It's harmless entertainment."

No. It's really not. It's a form of worship. It's the laying of our souls on an altar before a god who only wants to consume us. You are giving your heart to this god, and everything flows from the heart. Eventually the garbage makes its way downstream and comes to the surface.

It may look different than it did back then, but make no mistake about it: we shout, dance, and eventually bleed for this god, hoping for some kind of response. But the god of sexual pleasure always demands more.

In Romans 6:19, Paul describes sin as "ever-increasing." It happens with food. It happens with pornography or the need for more money. The gods keep demanding more. It's what is called the law of diminishing returns. Pleasure is always being promised around the next corner, after the next mile or the next sacrifice of your values. But the sacrifices cut deeper, and the satisfaction is ever more fleeting. "Midday passed, and they continued their frantic prophesying until the time for the evening sacrifice. But there was no response, no one answered, no one paid attention" (1 Kings 18:29).

There is no response. One of the saddest parts of my job is seeing people spend their lives worshiping a god that takes away everything and leaves them with nothing.

Roadways of the Mind

I'm sure that on the first day Amnon noticed Tamar's beauty and lusted after her it seemed harmless enough. After all, it wasn't like he was going to act on these feelings. It was just … *thinking.*

The battlefield of the gods is your heart. Your heart is shaped by your thoughts. Your thoughts determine who will win the throne for your heart. Proverbs 4:23 reads, "Above all else, guard your heart, for everything you do flows from it."

Let me reword that for you: be careful how you think, because that's what you will worship. That's why the Bible tells us to take every thought captive. What you think about ultimately has a lot to do with which god will win the war.

The battle begins in your mind, and it's not only the Bible that tells us so. Psychologists have given us increasing insight as to how that happens. During the last few decades, for example, the dominant movement in their field is what we call *cognitive psychology.* It examines how our thoughts shape our attitudes, emotions, and behavior.

Thoughts, attitudes, and emotions are all intertwined, but the mind is the starting point. Think about the effort of trying to carve a path through the woods. It's tiring and challenging. You cut out bushes, vines, and saplings, and the path is barely visible. But then people begin to use your path. The ground becomes a well-trodden path that looks as if it's been there forever.

Scientists tell us the brain works in this way. A new thought is like a blazed trail, and it's actually called a *neural pathway*. Children and teenagers are pushing back the wilderness of their young minds all the time, creating these roads of thought. The subject of sex is strange and challenging on first hearing, but then there is all the traffic of movies, music, reality TV, and school conversations, and the pathways twist into various parts of the woods.

Imagine a young lady whose neural pathways have been worn down by ideas that her value is established by the appearance of her body, the shape of this, the size of that. She begins to dress and to apply makeup based upon thousands of messages that she needs to have a certain kind of appeal — that, as a young woman, this is who she is.

Imagine a young man who has laid down his own mental highways. He ends up viewing pornography, and that particular neural pathway becomes the main road. In time, it's the default route for any thought about any woman he meets. And lustful thinking only reinforces those roads.

I've heard one psychologist explain that lust and self-pleasure are playing with neurochemical fire. He says that it results in a narcissistic and selfish approach to sexuality in which we bind ourselves to ourselves, if you will. Sexuality is meant to be relationship-based, not a private and selfish experience.

I read about a study in which a man sat and viewed pornographic images for a certain period of time each day, with a baseball cap on top of his computer monitor. After enough time elapsed, it was shown that, by association, he could be sexually aroused by the sight of a baseball cap. So the question is, Who or what am I binding myself to? What roads am I building or reinforcing in my mind? And where will those roads lead me? This is why idolatry is so dangerous. Our thoughts, our attitudes, and eventually our actions are determined by what we worship.

If you believe you can lock away your sexual thoughts in a special, airtight compartment, you've been taken in by a lie. The Bible tells us that "as he thinks in his heart, so *is* he" (Prov. 23:7 NKJV). The mind determines who we are and who we are becoming, and we think based on what we see and hear. What are you feeding your mind?

We're told to "take captive every thought to make it obedient to Christ" (2 Cor. 10:5). I love that metaphor of taking prisoners, because it's exactly what happens to our minds, one way or the other. We take it captive for truth or allow it to be seized and imprisoned by lies. Remember, this is war. The gods are at war for your soul.

Pleasure to Pain

When something good becomes a god, not only does pleasure disappear; we also experience pain.

Think through this with me. When we worship sex as a god, we find that it leads to the exact opposite of its divine design as a gift.

As a gift it brings connection; as a god it causes loneliness.

As a gift it brings pleasure; as a god it leads to emptiness.

As a gift it brings satisfaction; but as a god it demands slavery.

As a gift it brings intimacy; as a god, separation.

As a gift it brings unity; as a god it often causes divorce.

It's a beautiful gift and a tyrant of a god.

When pleasure becomes your god, you experience anything but. The god of pleasure is the master of bait and switch, luring us in with images and promises that become the chains and shackles of our mental imprisonment.

When we were living in California, my oldest daughter was four and she wanted a pet. I agreed, but there were a few conditions.

First, the pet had to be something that didn't bark, meow, or make any kind of noise. Second, the pet couldn't shed any kind of fur or hair. Third, the pet had to cost less than five bucks.

Within those limitations, we finally settled on a goldfish. When we went to purchase the fish, the sign offered a "three-day guarantee, no questions asked." This seemed like a safe policy and good stewardship for us.

So we took the fish — him, her, who knows? — home with us. My daughter named it Nemo and was eager to play with her new pet. But how do you play with a fish? You can't take it for a walk. You can't teach it to fetch. But you *can* take it swimming.

So we took a trip to the swimming pool with Nemo in a glass cup at the edge of the pool. While my daughter and I were splashing in the water, I noticed that Nemo was watching us. I figured the fish wanted to get out of the cup and into the vast ocean that this swimming pool must have seemed.

But I explained to my daughter that I wasn't too sure about that. There would be chemicals in the pool that might not be too good for Nemo. She was disappointed, but we moved on.

A while later, I was shocked to see that Nemo had moved on too. Nemo, living up to his name, had flip-flopped out of the cup and into the pool! I immediately started looking everywhere, trying to, you know ... find Nemo. I spotted him in the deep end of the pool, living large and taking charge, darting back and forth. You could almost hear the theme music in the background. I knew I had to catch the little fish very quickly.

Have you ever tried catching a goldfish in a swimming pool?

It's harder than it sounds.

All we could do finally was to wait the fish out. Nemo swam more and more slowly until the fish floated to the surface — belly up.*

---

*I did return Nemo to the store later that day. The same lady who sold me the fish was still on duty, and even though the sign said "No questions asked," she asked. I told her the truth: "The fish drowned."

I feel Nemo's pain. The water glass seemed so restrictive, and freedom looked so vast and enticing. And at first, once the fish dived in, it all felt so right. But what looked like pleasure was actually poison. The restriction turned out to be a loving thing, and "freedom" really meant destruction.

This is how the gods of pleasure work. What they offer is presented as freedom, as joy, but it's all toxic once you make the plunge. They tell you there's no way you can be happy within the restraints God has set up. Wild stallions have to run free, right? But the restraints are a design based on loving protection. The seat belt may cramp your style, and then save your life. The red traffic light makes you grumble, and then it fends off a terrible collision. The gods of pleasure don't like traffic signals, seat belts, or moments of caution. They tell you to stop worrying and go for it.

Amnon would tell you to buckle up and slow down because he discovered there wasn't any real or lasting pleasure. Just a quick release and then a whole lot of shame, pain, emptiness. He had to have known full well that actions had consequences. Tamar told her full brother, Absalom, what had happened. Absalom burned with rage, but he waited for his moment. Notice that he had an impulse to act on too; his happened to be a lust for revenge rather than sexual release. He served a god that was just as destructive.

Absalom waited two years before finding the right opportunity to have Amnon assassinated in revenge for raping his sister. Then chaos was in full reign. David, the father of these feuding sons, had to act, and it all boiled over into civil war. Absalom joined his half brother in the graveyard, and others died as well.

What if Amnon had the balance sheet that hindsight might have provided — what if any of us could ever enjoy that advantage? Amnon would have placed a fleeting moment of sensual pleasure on one side of the ledger, and his life — and terrible collateral damage — on the other. Why hadn't the whisper of lust, inside his mind, included all of that? Why was it all such a lie? Why was the bill so much more than he could afford to pay?

Worship is powerful. It has huge consequences, whether you praise the God of heaven or the god of appetite. If you worship God, it changes everything about you, and that creates positive ripples that echo into eternity. If you worship false gods, the ripples bring a little of hell to earth.

When we worship the Lord God with this area of our lives, we experience what we were really wanting all long — deep and intimate pleasure. When we turn his gift of sex into a god, it's only a matter of time until it breaks and stops doing what it was designed to do. But when the gift causes us to worship the giver, we discover that the giver gives us his gifts all the more abundantly.

Idol ID

How well do you control your thought life?

One study shows that men think about sex nineteen times per day, and women ten.[10]

The thoughts will come, particularly in a highly sexualized society. You're not going to avoid being exposed to a barrage of suggestive imagery unless you move into a monastery or convent. The god of sexual pleasure has set up temples everywhere.

We need to take control of our thoughts, submitting them to God along with everything else in our lives. And we do have a great deal of control over what we do with those thoughts once they occur to us. When a thought comes, we must make a choice.

Take inventory of your thought life. What does it tell you about yourself? Ask God to make you more conscious of what's on your mind, and to help you move your thinking in healthier directions. Remember Paul's advice: "Finally, brothers and sisters, whatever is true, whatever is noble, whatever is right, whatever is pure, whatever is lovely, whatever is admirable — if anything is excellent or praiseworthy — think about such things" (Phil. 4:8).

The best way to keep the bad things out is to fill 'er up with the good things. In other words, we don't just remove the god of sexual pleasure; we replace the god of sexual pleasure with the Lord God.

What sites do you visit on the internet when you're by yourself?

Within two decades, the internet has become the epicenter of our cultural sexual obsession. Think of the sites you visit as temples where you go to worship. This is another area over which we have control. Consider placing filters on your home computer, so that questionable sites aren't even an option.

What might be lacking in your intimacy with God?

The real issue, of course, is a spiritual one. Sometimes people seek fantasies and pursuits of various kinds in an effort to fill a gap in their spirits. What is it we really need? What is it we think we're after when we look at imagery or chase fantasies?

Take inventory of where you stand with God these days. Is he real to you — a daily presence in your life? Where is he in your thoughts when the temptations come? Do you believe he has the power to rescue you?

Jesus taught his disciples to pray, "Lead us not into temptation, but deliver us from the evil one" (Matt. 6:13).

Ask God to lead you to places and situations where you won't be tempted. Remember that he is always there, and will never leave you nor forsake you. Visualize his presence during the most trying moments. Draw near to God, and he will draw near to you.

The ultimate path away from a false god is the path toward the true one.

CHOOSING JESUS:

Jesus My Satisfaction

*Idols are defeated not by being removed
but by being replaced.*

The god of sex promised us satisfaction, yet he left us lonely and ashamed.

He lured and enticed us by distorting what was designed to be a gift and a blessing. He made it seem as if nothing could be more satisfying than the quick release of physical urges. Yet nothing could have left us feeling smaller and weaker—as if those urges defined who we were, as if we were beasts of the field and no more.

Then we came to Jesus, who offers the greatest joy imaginable—so much greater and fuller than any physical impulse. We could see for the first time that the pursuit of the god of sex was never about love at all. It reduced others to mere objects to be used for our personal pleasure. But the love of Jesus finds its greatest satisfaction in service rather than use of others. It exalts them. It affirms them as children of God. It connects with them in body, soul, mind, and spirit, rather than simple base instinct.

Jesus is our satisfaction. All along, it was intimacy we really wanted, and he gives us that. When we have a love relationship with him, an unending honeymoon commences. Christ grows more wonderful to us every day.

Not that sex is put aside. On the contrary, it takes on a beauty and resonance we never could have imagined — the opposite of shame. We have been designed so that the level of intimacy we can have with our spouse is directly related to the depth of intimacy we have with Christ. Sexual intimacy as God designed it takes a human relationship to a whole new level, because we're not using one another; we're delighting in one another. The god of sex dehumanized us; Christ restores our wholeness and makes the two of us one flesh — so much the greater than the sum of our parts — as we seek him together.

The god of sex offers a counterfeit joy that becomes more elusive through time, ever harder to please, ever closer to emptiness. But the love of Christ only opens up to deeper joys, becoming ever greater.

Sexual pleasure, rightly viewed, is a rich gift that shows how much God loves us. But its ecstasy is only a foretaste of divine glory, a hint of the eternal pleasure of knowing, loving, and serving Christ. He is our true satisfaction.

chapter 7

the god
of entertainment

See if you can imagine this one.

People arrive hours early for church. On Sunday mornings, they don't just set a backup alarm clock to assure they wake up in time; they set a backup for the backup. They arrange their schedules to make sure they don't miss gathering for worship. Throughout the week, they talk about what happened on the previous Sunday as excitement builds for the upcoming church service.

There are all-day talk shows on the radio devoted to reviewing last week's service and breaking down the next one. There's even a TV show called "ChurchCenter" that runs highlight clips of church activities that have happened across the nation that day.

When Sunday comes, the members start loading up their trucks, SUVs, and sedans hours before the service starts.

"Hurry," says Dad frantically. "We're behind again."

"It's 6:00 a.m." says Mom. "Church doesn't start for five hours."

"Last time we left at this time, we had to park three miles from the sanctuary and sit in the nosebleed seats. Someday, I really want to sit in the front row. But you have to camp out on the church lawn to have any chance of that."

The roads are really congested on the way to church, no matter how early you leave. At church, there are vehicles parked as far as the eye can see, and folks are out tailgating. Some have elaborate spreads prepared, breaking out portable grills and lawn chairs in the church parking lot. Some have television monitors and satellite dishes so they can catch updates from other worship services while they wait for their own.

It's nice weather today, not that it matters. Even in the dead of winter, they'll be out here in the same numbers. The masses begin filing into the sanctuary, cheering with great passion and excitement.

Once the service starts, the people are all on their feet — not that they ever sit down. Of course, a bunch of young guys are in the front row. They've probably been here since Friday night. They have no shirts, and each one has a letter on his chest. Together they spell GET YOUR TITHE ON. Apparently the rumor has gotten out that the pastor is indeed going to teach on biblical stewardship and worshiping God with our money. Everyone is *pumped* for the giving sermon. It's one of the highlights of the year.

After several hours, people start looking at their watches. Everyone is thinking the same thing: "I hope the sermon goes into overtime!"

The Church That Peyton Built

I'm sure you're picking up on my not-so-subtle point. The above scenario seems beyond crazy to us, but if you take out church and put in football, then it seems perfectly sane.

A few years ago, my youngest daughter wanted nothing more than to go to a Colts football game in Indianapolis. That's the only thing she asked for at Christmas. Her main present that year was a pair of Colts tickets, wrapped up in a Peyton Manning jersey. Since she was only ten at the time, someone needed to take her, and I was willing to make that sacrifice. The truth is, I'm a huge sports fan, and she came by her NFL devotion honestly.

It was a Sunday afternoon game, but we drove down on Saturday evening to make sure we would be at the stadium in plenty of time. We woke up early on Sunday and went to a local church. She begged me to let her wear her Peyton Manning jersey to the worship service, but I told her that people wouldn't be wearing Colts gear to church.

I have never been more wrong in my life.

We sat in the back and gazed upon a sea of blue. There were thirty-seven people wearing Peyton Manning jerseys. She counted. Two people had their faces painted.

A few hours later, I was sitting among eighty thousand fans in Lucas Oil Stadium, and, yes, I had my own face painted. We both cheered until we lost our voices. We made a great memory and had a blast. But on the drive home, as my exhausted daughter slept, I couldn't help but think about the fact that I had really attended two worship services that day. The question I was asking myself was, Which one was I most passionate about?

It wouldn't be hard to make a case that our cultural obsession with entertainment is essentially a surrogate religion. But let's stay with sports specifically for a moment. Charles S. Prebish, a professor of religious studies at Pennsylvania State University, doesn't believe our passion for it is *like* a religion. He flat-out says it *is* one: "America's newest and fastest-growing religion, far outdistancing whatever is in second place."[11]

Its temples are the great stadiums that are sacred ground to many, sites of weekend pilgrimages. Its priests are in the zebra stripes. Its gods wear their names on the back of their jerseys. Its liturgy is fan chants, and its sacrifices are the vast amounts of money that fans pay for tickets and team gear.

But the god of the pigskin isn't the only entertainment deity. How about the world of celebrities and the incredible amount of attention that people devote to showbiz couples and activities?

We have celebrities who are famous for being movie or TV or music stars. Then we have people who are famous simply for being famous. Fans are transfixed by the daily life of Kim Kardashian or the latest struggles of Lindsey Lohan. Celebrity news publications often dominate the magazine aisle, filled with pictures of celebrities doing things like going to the grocery store or taking their dog for a walk. It's not what they're doing that's so compelling; it's just who they are.

Gamers

If you know any teenagers, you may understand that the god of video games is on the ascent. Some aficionados spend several days at a time immersed in virtual worlds defined by computer pixels, their true identities lost in the impersonations of elves or ninja warriors. I shudder to think how many hours I've spent trying to knock down whatever strange shack the Angry Birds are chirping about.

Some enthusiasts, known as "extreme gamers," spend forty-eight hours per week in the glare of a monitor, begrudgingly leaving the screen only to visit the bathroom or get another energy drink. Nearly one in ten kids between the ages of eight and eighteen could be classified as clinically addicted to video games.[12] Their brains are wired to need more and more of the unique stimulus of the game, releasing enough of the pleasure-inducing dopamine to hook the gamer.

A fifteen-year-old video game addict is described as displaying "all the characteristics of a heroin addict. You haven't got someone putting a needle in their arm and having a high, but you've got all the telltale collateral damage of a heroin addict: withdrawal from his family, withdrawal from his friends, lies to cover his addiction. He'll do anything."[13]

What about the amount of time we spend on social networks like Facebook? John Piper put it this way, "One of the great uses of Twitter and Facebook will be to prove at the Last Day that prayerlessness was not from lack of time."* The Lord God has often lost out when competing with the gods of entertainment for our time and attention.

I'll tell you the moment that convinced me we had a problem. A few years ago, one of my friends traveled to India on a mission trip. After he returned, he was excited to show me the pictures and tell me about his journey. It's always interesting to see the everyday lives of people from other cultures. My friend had a picture of what was essentially the family room in an Indian home. The centerpiece, what we'd think of as the mantle on the hearth, featured a carved idol. He pointed out that every seat in the room was carefully arranged so that it was facing this idol.

I shook my head sadly at the sight of a family with a false god at the very center of its world. A few hours later, I walked in the front door of my house and had a seat in my recliner. I grabbed the remote, turned on the TV, and kicked back in the chair. Suddenly it hit me. My eyes scanned the room slowly, and sure enough every seat in our room was carefully positioned to face the fifty-inch flat screen on my mantel.

Don't get me wrong, I'm not anti-entertainment. I'm just wondering if we've gone from watching it to worshiping it.

Maybe you think, Worshiping? Really? Aren't you getting a little carried away?

Well, consider that the average American watches more than four-and-a-half hours of television every day. In the average home in the US, the set is on for more than eight hours and it offers more than one hundred channels. At your office, when people gather around the water cooler, what subject aligns their conversation? What does your family spend the most time doing together? For years, television has been the answer to these questions.

Our own false gods tend to be invisible to us; I can probably see

* Yep, he tweeted that: *twitter.com/johnpiper.*

yours, but I'll miss detecting my own. Here's a clue: discover what the chairs of your heart are aligned around.

Around what does everything orbit in your life? What are the locked-in dates on your calendar, the essential items in your budget?

Some families have shrines to their football teams — rooms decked out in school colors, devoted to framed memorabilia and souvenirs from games. Others are dominated by imagery of Elvis Presley or with some kind of collection: electric trains, baseball cards, even Hummel figurines. My point is that we may shake our heads sadly at the family in India, but we should at least consider the possibility that we have our own home shrines.

And Now the Good News

Okay, I feel the need to push the pause button at this point, because I fear that this may all begin to sound a little legalistic. I'm not trying to construct a tower of rules on this, nor saying that entertainment is evil. Far from it. Like food and sex, entertainment is a gift from God — something that can be good until we turn it into a god.

After all, how can you not be entertained by God's creation? How can we avoid the conclusion that he entertained himself by putting the world, the stars, and the galaxies together? How do you think he intends us to respond to a rainbow or a mountain range or a seashore? He didn't just give us a bare, functional place to live; he gave us a planet of wonders.

And what did he expect people to do on that seventh day of rest that he commanded? We can't sleep for twenty-four hours. Entertainment can be rest for the mind and emotions.

How do you think he intended us to respond to the dignified penguin, the playful kitten, the dog who insists you throw him the stick?

If entertainment is wrong, why did God make snow so much fun? Why do people in every human culture have the ability to laugh and be amused?

He is a God of joy, and he wants us to know that joy. He "richly provides us with everything for our enjoyment" (1 Tim. 6:17).

And think of Jesus, who taught through stories and amusing snippets of life. The story of the prodigal son is often considered the greatest short story ever told. His parables were powerful for teaching because they were powerfully entertaining.

What's the problem with entertainment, then?

Solomon, one of the greatest figures of the Old Testament, found the answer to that question. He pursued entertainment relentlessly, looking for pleasure.

He chased after it as hard and as fast as he could. Solomon was the king of Israel, the son of King David. The Old Testament book of Ecclesiastes is basically the journal he kept while he pursued pleasure. In one of his early entries he writes, "I said to myself, 'Come now, I will test you with pleasure to find out what is good'" (Eccl. 2:1).

Solomon has incredible wealth and power, and he spares no expense in trying to entertain himself. He begins with laughter. He tunes into the comedy channel and hires the Jerry Seinfeld of his day as a court jester. But he soon concludes that it's meaningless. There's no lasting joy in it.

He tries the life of partying, but sees the emptiness of it quickly. He entertains himself by taking on great projects. He builds houses, plants vineyards, and creates parks. He is a man of many disciplines and interests, trying to find which, if any, will fill the void in his soul.

He has the luxury of all this experimentation because he's vastly wealthy. He has servants, butlers, maids, chauffeurs, massage therapists, personal shoppers, and even ongoing live entertainment.

Ecclesiastes 2:8 tells us that he brought in a choir of men and women — and of course, a harem.

Most people have heard about the harem — all the wives and concubines. There are women from every nation, food from every culture, books of wisdom from every civilization. Solomon covers all the bases. He's going to find pleasure if it kills him!

And how does it end? With this exclamation: "Meaningless! Meaningless! ... Utterly meaningless! Everything is meaningless" (Eccl. 1:2).

Nothing was particularly wrong with the entertainment — minus 999 of the women. So what was Solomon's problem? He was trying to make it something it wasn't. He was looking for the meaning of life in amusement, trying to find the main event in what was just the sideshow.

Spoiler Alert

Solomon gives us a heads up on where pursuing pleasure will ultimately lead us. We've seen this bait-and-switch tactic before in the temples of the gods. They offer us the sky and give us the mud. Food becomes insatiable hunger; sex becomes shame; entertainment becomes restless boredom.

Have you ever wondered why so many people are bored today, during an age of technological wonders, of over two hundred TV channels? Science writer Winifred Gallagher believes that boredom is largely a recent problem that is absent from many other cultures. She describes a Western scholar who has lived among the bushmen of Africa for years and has become fluent in their language. He has tried over the years to come up with an equivalent to the word *boredom* in their language, but there is a disconnect; they don't understand the concept. The closest they can come to it is *tired*. Our word *boredom* didn't appear in English until the

Industrial Age. Yep, that's about the time modern entertainment began to evolve.[14]

And yet the word *amusement* actually comes from the world of worship. *Amusement* has as its root the word *muse*. The Muses were the female Greek gods who were said to inspire great writing, science, and artistic achievement. They were gods of reflection. When we add the *a* as a prefix, it brings in the idea of "lacking." So *a*musement is the lack of inspiration, the lack of reflection.[15]

We seek amusements because we don't want to think. Haven't you ever wandered into the living room after a hard day and just wanted to vegetate, to watch something mindless? That's fine, up to a point. But don't miss this truth: instead of inspiring our bored and apathetic existence, the god of entertainment makes us even more that way. Have you ever had a Solomon moment in which you watched your fourth straight "reality show" or flipped through hundreds of channels and concluded "there is nothing on!" What you're really saying is "Meaningless, meaningless! Utterly meaningless!"

Instead of being entertained, we increasingly become the opposite — bored.

Chasing After the Wind

Solomon pursued pleasure and entertainment and here is his conclusion: "I have seen all the things that are done under the sun; all of them are meaningless, a chasing after the wind" (Eccl. 1:14).

Put this book down, go outside, and take three minutes to chase the wind.

Are you back? How'd that go for you? What do you have to show for it?

A few years ago, Neil Postman wrote a book called *Amusing Ourselves to Death*. He argued that popular culture is dumbing down our world at a startlingly fast rate. His title captures the

121

power of the god of entertainment. It promises us life, but takes our life from us one thirty-minute sitcom at a time. Solomon pursued pleasure and entertainment, and he concludes that it's meaningless, but he also gives some more specific symptoms. "Generations come and generations go, but the earth remains forever. The sun rises and the sun sets, and hurries back to where it rises. The wind blows to the south and turns to the north; round and round it goes, ever returning on its course. All streams flow into the sea, yet the sea is never full. To the place the streams come from, there they return again. All things are wearisome, more than one can say. The eye never has enough of seeing, nor the ear its fill of hearing" (Eccl. 1:4 – 8).

Solomon seems to say, "It just wears me out. You work hard and what do you have to show for it? I mean really." He uses the rotation of the earth and weather patterns as examples of how he feels about life. It's like we're just spinning in circles.

He wrote these words before the internet, iPods, and satellite TV. Never in the history of humanity has there been so much entertainment and so little satisfaction.

Solomon does offer a particular, interesting phrase twenty-nine times in his book. It defines the parameters of his search: "under the sun." He has been looking everywhere under the sun. He has seen many things under the sun. He has found no meaning under the sun. No wonder he's tired and frustrated. His sights are set too low; his parameters are too narrow. What he's really searching for is out there, but it isn't under the sun.

C. S. Lewis captured it this way, "Creatures are not born with desires unless satisfaction for those desires exists. A baby feels hunger ... well, there is such a thing as food. A duckling wants to swim; there is such a thing as water." He goes on to say, "If I find in myself a desire which no experience in this world can satisfy, the most probable explanation is that I was made for another world. If none of my earthly pleasures satisfy it, that does not prove the universe is a fraud. Probably earthly pleasures were never meant to satisfy it but only to arouse it, to suggest the real thing."[16]

Ultimately the gods of pleasure can't satisfy our desires. We come to final realization that what we need cannot be found through the stomach, through sexuality, or through amusement. We want pure, unadulterated joy, and the trail finally leads to God himself. At the end of Solomon's diary, he reaches this conclusion: "That's the whole story. Here now is my final conclusion: Fear God and obey his commands, for this is everyone's duty" (Eccl. 12:13 NLT).

We were made for God, and until he is our greatest pleasure, all the other pleasures of this life will lead to emptiness. Augustine expressed this in his prayer nearly fifteen centuries ago: "Our hearts are restless until they find rest in thee."

In the middle of the last century, A. W. Tozer wrote about the restless heart in an essay called "The Great God Entertainment." He said that the more vibrant our inner lives are, the less we need from the outside — that is, the more active we are in mind and spirit, the less we need to fall back on external media and other input.

By that measure, he said, "The present inordinate attachment to every form of entertainment is evidence that the inner life of modern man is in serious decline."[17] And this was the 1950s! I'd really rather not hear what his opinion would be of this generation.

There is a place in life for relaxation through various forms of entertainment, including sports, television, movies, music, and games, but the question is, Do we seek to fill the spiritual vacuum inside us with empty entertainment, or is it the empty entertainment that is creating the vacuum? I suppose it's the chicken-and-egg question. But there's plenty of evidence that our increasing reliance on the flash and glamour of our entertainment is blinding us to quieter and truer pleasure.

Power Off

So how do we smash these idols? How do we kick them off the heart's throne? Often it's as easy as turning the power off.

I'll never forget the first time I went to a church service in Haiti. I had heard from other friends who'd made similar mission trips about worship services lasting four to six hours. It caught my attention; I was impressed with that level of commitment.

Most preachers in the States would tell you that they start losing people if the church service goes much longer than an hour. There's also the pressure to make sure that hour is filled with enough song-and-dance and multimedia to hold attention.

So when I got to Haiti, I spoke to the local Haitian pastor about the time differences in our services. I said, "What is it about the Haitian people that keeps them worshiping at church for so many hours?" It was a mystery to me, and I was hoping for a profound answer that would redefine my ecclesiology. Here's how he responded. He laughed and said, "In Haiti, we have nothing else to do."

I laughed, but then I was almost immediately struck by the weight of his answer. They didn't have televisions, radios, phones, computers, theaters — the Lord God didn't have much competition. And then I realized the implications of that.

What if you "went Haitian" for a week or two? What if you had a media fast, other than the requirements of your work?

Can I challenge you to eliminate God's competition, just for a test, and see what happens?

Turn off the TV.

Log off Facebook.

Turn down the music.

Unplug the game console.

Turn your eyes to the Lord.

Idol ID

What are your favorite forms of entertainment?

Spend some time thinking about your leisure diet. Is it filled with cultural "junk food," or do you watch high-quality movies, read well-written books, listen to edifying music, and look for intelligent TV broadcasts?

Which ones take up most of your time? And given your answer, what insights do your choices offer as to who you really are?

What forms of entertainment have most affected your worldview?

What cultural or pop cultural works have been the most influential for you? Why?

Where and when have you exhibited the most passion and excitement?

For example, those who attend rock concerts tend to show high levels of emotion as various songs are played. Sports enthusiasts cry, sing, and even create riots — not just in the US but across the world at events such as the World Cup.

At what venues have you been the most emotionally engaged? How would you compare it to a worship experience?

What kinds of entertainment media have you found to be the most addictive?

Many people are simply hooked on the internet, spending hour after hour browsing websites, "Facebooking," or pursuing other online opportunities. Others are addicted to daytime soaps or reality TV shows. Some people can't bear to be without their phones or their iPods. Entertainment can be as addictive as food, alcohol, or anything else.

If you were marooned on a desert island, what forms of entertainment would you miss the most?
Stated another way, which media would you struggle hardest to give up here and now? If there is one you couldn't stand to do without, what does that suggest about its place in your life?

Jesus My Passion

*Idols are defeated not by being removed
but by being replaced.*

The god of entertainment promised us a circus. And in our adult world, which can be gray and drab, filled with obligations and responsibilities, that sounded pretty good.

We looked for attractions and surprises and amusements to create in us a sense of wonder. Maybe we would find it in music or in movies or in games or in sports. The god of entertainment was hawking them all, like a carnival barker: "Step right up! Be amazed, be amused! Come one! Come all!"

But in the end, the music was flat, the movies were formulaic, and the games were rigged. The circus would leave town and we wait impatiently for another one to take its place.

Then we found our passion in Jesus. If you haven't

experienced it for yourself, I get that it sounds ridiculous — how could a dusty old Bible character compete with big-budget movies or action-packed games or soulful tunes? But once you know Jesus and passionately pursue him, it seems ridiculous that we thought we could ever find what we wanted on a movie screen, a website, or a playlist.

Jesus said in John 10:10, "I have come that they may have life, and have it to the full."

part 3

the temple
of power

chapter 8

the god
of success

When people talked about Chuck Bentley, the word *driven* always came up. It seems he was born ambitious.

By the time he finished school, he was ready to seek his fortune in the world. He was already thinking, "How can I make a name for myself? I'll do whatever it takes to be successful."

He understood that business made the world go round. Business drove everything. Yet now there was something driving business itself. It was called the internet.

This was the 1990s, boom time in cyberspace. The web was the new California gold rush. So Chuck loaded up the wagons and headed west.

He started a company called OfficeExchange. It was built around the future of the internet, and from there it was all green lights and greenbacks. Investors were chasing internet startups with something approaching hysteria, and it took Chuck no more than a couple of weeks to raise more than a million dollars to get his company up and running.

He was a young man with founder stock, with options and benefits and a future that was deep and wide. A venture forum in Silicon Valley named Chuck's idea as one of the sixty best seed-stage companies in the world. Six months after launch, he was presenting his idea before fifteen hundred venture capital investors.

What a ride. While most of his friends were pursuing money,

Chuck knew that money was pursuing him. He sat back to take a breath and thought, "I'm the next Amazon.com. I'm the next eBay."

What he felt wasn't really about the money — it was almost comical how easily the financing had come. Money was just a way of keeping score. What Chuck was high on was something bigger: success. He was going to stand out. He was going to be a name — like Yahoo, like AOL — an iconic brand synonymous with the dot-com age. The hype was his heroin. He needed a fix daily.

Lying in bed at the end of a sixteen-hour day, he told Ann, his wife, "If we went public at ten dollars a share, I would be a multimillionaire. Can you imagine that?"

Ann didn't have a lot to say, and it puzzled Chuck. She wasn't nearly as jazzed about all this as he was.

"Don't worry about it changing me," he said. "I'll always be humble. Listen, if we got to a hundred per share, I'll just buy us a sports franchise or two — give our money something to do, right?"

Ann wasn't so comfortable with all the bravado. Her husband did seem to be changing. Who was he becoming? It was a little frightening. He worked seven days per week, most of his waking hours. He was absolutely driven by the IPO (initial public offering) and how it would play out.

When he was around, he wasn't really around. His eyes told the story of a man who was elsewhere, or several different elsewheres, a man who would make furtive glances at the telephone and keep checking his email as if it were an itch he couldn't help but scratch.

Something powerful had stolen her husband away from her. The odd thing about it was that he was so *lit up* by it all. It was like some new kind of drug. Any observer would have to say he was happy, motivated, riding the adrenaline wave.

Except he wasn't … well, *Chuck*. She knew it; the children knew it. Was this the price of success? Would he have to sacrifice his family, even himself, on the altar of success?

King of the Hill

The god of success has no problem finding followers.

He is attractive, compelling, charismatic. He walks into your everyday, rat-race world and shows you what life could be at the top of the heap. And what he's selling is hard to ignore. He offers us the applause and envy that makes life sweet.

This god gives us a line as old as the garden of Eden: "You can run the whole thing. It's your life, so why shouldn't you be at the wheel? Why not put the pedal down and see how fast you can get to the finish line?"

He plays on the most basic problem of humanity — that pull toward doing it our way, aka *pride.*

The gods of success are all about personal achievement, rewards we chase and get for ourselves. Is life going to be good? Are we going to be satisfied? The gods of success give us very convenient ways to keep score: the title after our name, the sum on our paycheck, the square footage of the new house. We put our hope and find our identity in what the god of success offers. And so we climb and claw our way to the top.

Did you play a game in grade school called King of the Hill? Or maybe you called it King of the Mountain. When I was in the fourth grade, we played that game every day at recess. It went like this: all the boys would push and shove each other to the ground, and when the whistle blew, whoever was left standing on the hill was crowned king.

My guess is that most schools have outlawed such games these days, because of the sheer brutality. I loved this game. You know why? Because I was the undisputed, undefeated king of the hill.*

I was enjoying my reign as king, and then one day we got a new

---

*Full disclosure: I was the same size in the fourth grade as I am now and was already shaving.

student in our class. This student was bigger and taller than me, and worst of all, this student was a girl!

At first, I didn't sweat it. I thought, What self-respecting girl would ever want to play King of the Hill? But I hadn't reckoned on this girl being Barbara.*

Barbara wore cowgirl boots. She made fun of the girls in our class who wore braids. I knew I was in trouble when we were sitting in art class on her second day of school and Barbara ate glue. I'd heard about glue-eaters from other schools, but this was my first real-life encounter.

Sure enough, at recess that day, Barbara wanted to play King of the Hill. In hindsight, it would have been sensible to have a "no girls allowed" rule. I would contend that not having this rule wasn't an oversight, because we weren't playing Queen of the Hill, or Intergender Overlord of the Hill. This was *King* of the Hill. It was implied. It's like a men's restroom. A sign saying girls aren't allowed isn't necessary because by definition they are excluded. I digress.

I tried politely explaining this to Barbara. But you can hang this on a wall, sew it into a pillow, and post it on Facebook: there is no reasoning with a glue-eater. Barbara dug her boots into the ground and came after me. When the whistle blew that day, I was no longer king. I had been dethroned by a girl. I still remember what a horrible feeling that was. The rest of my fourth grade year, I was consumed with plots to dethrone the evil queen and reclaim my rightful place. Thankfully, Barbara lost interest and turned her attention to bullying the kids on the playground.

I've discovered that King of the Hill isn't just a childhood game we play, but often ends up becoming our life's pursuit: do whatever it takes to make it to the top.

In Luke 18, Jesus has a conversation with a king of the hill.

---

*Hey, Barbara, if you are reading this — I'm talking about a different Barbara.

That's not exactly what he's called, but pretty close. He is described by three words: *rich, young,** *ruler.* He was a man who had accomplished, achieved, and accumulated. He was the very definition of success. Nothing wrong with that, unless those were the things he was living for.

Luke 18:18 reads, "A certain ruler asked him, 'Good teacher, what must I do to inherit eternal life?'"

Pay attention to that question. In essence, he wants to know what he must do to be successful. That's a good question to ask Jesus, but did you notice where he puts the emphasis? He asks, "What must I do to *inherit?*"

The Greek word for inherit could also be translated as "acquire" or "earn." Verbs reveal a lot, don't they? This man is assuming that eternal life is something he can achieve, something he can add to his résumé. It's a red flag signaling that the god of success might be the king of the hill in someone's life. It's looking at things and thinking, "I can grab that."

For this rich young ruler, salvation is one more trophy, an earned reward. Worshiping the gods of success isn't just about secular accomplishments and commendations. It's not just getting caught up with job titles and social status. In fact one of the most common gods of success is the worship of religious rules. We put our trust in our own mastery of rule-keeping.

The god of success invites you to save yourself instead of depending upon Jesus to do it. This is one of the reasons I believe the most successful of people often have the hardest of times becoming followers of Christ. Being a devoted disciple means they must acknowledge their own helplessness and their ultimate need

---

* Matthew's gospel specifically describes him this way. This will be hard for some of you to hear, but biblically speaking, *young* is a reference to someone under forty. Therefore, if you're over forty, *young* is no longer a word that the Bible would apply to you. If you still claim that adjective, you are being unbiblical. I apologize if you had to put on your bifocals to read this footnote.

—the need for rescue. It's not easy for a successful person to admit the need for help.

This is why Bill Maher, the TV pundit, says this of the crucifixion: "I just don't get it. The thought of someone else cleansing me of my sins is ridiculous. I don't need anyone to cleanse me. I can cleanse myself."

This is why Warren Buffett, after donating 85 percent of his forty-four billion dollars to charity, would say, "There is more than one way to get to heaven, but this is a great way."

Sure, it *would* be a great way: just save up enough bucks, brownie points, box tops, soup labels, or Chuck E. Cheese tickets and redeem them at the golden gate. That makes sense to us, because life as we know it is all about earning things, making our own way. If you want something, you work for it. You pay for everything in blood, sweat, and tears, and economic systems are always based on getting what you pay for.

In most walks of life, that's a good system. When it comes to guilt, however, there's one problem: sin has put all of us hopelessly in debt. We'll never be successful enough. There are not enough deeds or donations in the world to buy an ounce of the purity we need.

So in God's economy, success only comes when we declare spiritual bankruptcy.

Back to the rich young ruler. He wants to know what he must do to be successful, and Jesus replies, in so many words, "You know the commandments, right?"

This is exactly the answer the successful man wanted. He bursts out that he's kept all the commandments since he was a boy. The commands were a checklist, a list of merit badges that he had devoted himself to. Through hard work and determination, he has kept the rules. Add *spiritual* as a fourth word to describe his success. He was the rich, young, spiritual ruler.

The Bible tells us that Jesus "looked at him and loved him" (Mark 10:21). He did so even as he observed, "One thing you lack."

And then he dropped the bomb.

Jesus told him to sell all his possessions and give the money to the poor, thus accumulating treasure *in heaven*. I wish I could've seen this guy's face when Jesus told him to sell all that he had. Picture Gary Coleman from *Diff'rent Strokes* saying, "Whatchoo talkin' 'bout, Willis?"

This wasn't the standard prescription from Jesus. This was a particular word for a particular individual. In fact, in Luke 19, Jesus makes no such requirement of Zaccheaus, an evil tax collector who repents. So why does Jesus go so hardcore here?

Here's why: he looks into the heart of this passionate, successful young man, so well-dressed and energetic and well-meaning, and he sees that the Lord isn't on the throne. So Jesus puts himself in direct competition with the man's trophies of success. He says, "You choose."

The young man couldn't do it. "At this the man's face fell. He went away sad, because he had great wealth" (Mark 10:22).

His face fell. He doesn't seem to have taken much time to mull it over. He abruptly turned and sadly walked away, much like a kid at a carnival who walks up to the best ride in the park but discovers it will cost him all the money he has.

The rich young ruler had come to define himself by his success and accomplishments, whether they were counted in cash or commandments. He knew that no matter how much he wanted to go after Jesus, there was a price he would not pay; there was a god he could not overthrow.

Jesus exclaimed, "How hard it is for the rich to enter the kingdom of God!" (Mark 10:23).

I can imagine the sadness in Jesus' eyes as he said it. He loved that young man who had come after him with bright eyes and left in dejection. But Jesus doesn't chase him down and say, "Hey, hold up! Did I say 'everything'? You don't have to sell *everything*. I'm sure we can come to some kind of arrangement." Jesus doesn't treat this as a negotiation.

For some people, the idea of standing before God without an impressive résumé is unthinkable. We want to show him our success, prove our worth. But to God, success is precisely the opposite of that. It's being willing to step away from all the stuff, all the achievements, and say, "None of that means a thing to me, Lord. I lay it all before you; you and only you are my success."

Cost Analysis

Chuck, the new internet tycoon, couldn't understand where his wife was coming from. What had gotten into Ann?

Like many guys, he was wired to be a provider. His job was to feed and shelter his wife and children. And the way he saw it, he was hitting a home run with the bases loaded when it came to that. He was going to have mansions and fast cars and European vacations and the best private schools for the kids. What was not to like?

Ann felt it was fine to have a strong drive, until it began driving a wedge into the family's togetherness. "Your children don't really see you anymore," she said. "Even I don't see you. Is it worth that kind of sacrifice?"

She talked about their spiritual goals. He thought about that and had to admit that he didn't have any specific ones. On the other hand, he and God had a deal. If God would give Chuck enormous success, then he would give God all the glory.

It seemed to him like a pretty fair exchange. Yet something deep inside was nagging at him, telling him that he was losing his way.

About that time, he had another conversation, and the subject of goals came up. A friend said, "I believe people with goals are the ones who go places in life." Chuck agreed. He said that he was a man of goals too, and asked his friend what his were.

The friend said, "You have to write them down. They're not real if they're not written." And he opened his wallet and began reading from a list. One of them was to have a gold presidential Rolex watch. "I'm going to have that by the end of this year," he said, "and I also know what it's going to cost me."

"So how much?" Chuck figured he would hear a dollar figure.

"Less time with my family," his friend replied matter-of-factly. "That's my price. It's going to be more evenings, more weekends, more work."

Simple as that. And he returned to his list. "I want to be a member of the most exclusive country club," he said. "That one will cost me giving up some hobbies and one family vacation annually."

Chuck's friend spoke casually, even contentedly about the prices he was going to pay. He was more than willing to make these sacrifices. He was that far down a road that Chuck realized he was now walking himself.

Chuck revisited his personal goals. They really weren't so very different, other than the fact that he hadn't been so brutally honest about counting the cost. Something inside was wanting to know, "Why is it all about money and prestige and fame? What am I really sacrificing for these things? Where does God fit into any of it?"

He eased his conviction and said to himself, God and I, we have a deal. I get the success; he gets the credit.

But he was starting to see a flaw in his thinking. Maybe God wasn't happy with just coming in later and taking a bow; maybe he wanted to be in Chuck's mind and heart *now*.

God might want to be a controlling partner and not just an investor.

TUBES AND TEENS

In 2011, a team of UCLA psychologists studied the values of TV characters in the shows most popular with preteens over the years. For example, *Andy Griffith* and *Lucy* from the sixties; *Happy Days* characters and *Laverne and Shirley* from the seventies; and *American Idol* and *Hannah Montana* from recent times.

The most frequent value of contemporary shows was found to be "fame." Between 1967 and 1997, the top value had been "community feeling, or being part of a group." That value suddenly dropped to eleventh place. The second most frequent value from 1967, "being kind and helpful to others," had plunged from second to thirteenth place.

The predominant message of today's preteen shows seems to be that a successful life is all about finding a way to be famous.

One of the researchers said, "I was shocked, especially by the dramatic changes in the last ten years.... If you believe that television reflects the culture, as I do, then American culture has changed drastically."[*]

[*] Stuart Wolpert, "Popular TV Shows Teach Children Fame Is Most Important Value, UCLA Psychologists Report," *UCLA Newsroom* (July 11, 2011), *newsroom.ucla.edu/portal/ucla/popular-tv-shows-teach-children-210119.aspx* (accessed May 9, 2012).

Keeping Score

What are we talking about when we say *success*? It's one of those words that could have a slightly different shade of meaning for each of us. We tend to attach it to a personal goal or objective.

Sociologists tell us that our culture defines success as the prestige that comes from attaining an elevated social status. It's winning a big, public game of King of the Hill. Your hill might be slightly different than mine, but there's a broad consensus today about the ingredients that add up to success.

In the next chapter we'll explore the god of money. What he offers is far more simple: personal wealth, buying power. There's plenty of allure there. But his associate and fellow god of power, success, wants us to bow down to a *position* in society — a pecking order, if you will. Money is certainly a component of that, because that's what we most often use to keep score. For most of us, it's a key ingredient to success, but it's not just about money. It's about prestige and clout. It's about respect and recognition. It's about having the right seat at the table, the right space in the parking lot, the right title on the business card, and the right clothes in the closet. It's about getting the watch, the trophy, the promotion, or the award.

Success is finding out how the score is kept, and then scoring.

The word *success* is not found very frequently in the Scriptures, but one of the closest biblical equivalents is the word *blessed*. In ancient Greek culture, this term was used to signify "the state of happiness and well-being such as the gods enjoy."[18] Even today, we use that word as the more humble way of saying, "I'm successful." A guest comes by and says, "You have a beautiful home. I love your sports cars and your yacht." You smile modestly and say, "I've been blessed."

So think about the difference between these two words, *success* and *blessed*. *Success* is a word we use to speak of something that we have done and accomplished. The circumstances of your life can be the same, but the word *blessed* is an indication not that you have done something, but that something has been done for you.

Let me put it this way: success is when we achieve; blessed is when we receive. If we say "I'm successful," we are giving the glory to ourselves. When we say "I'm blessed," we are giving the glory to God.

Jesus gives an in-depth portrait of what it means to be blessed when he begins the Sermon on the Mount. Beginning in Matthew 5, Jesus gives a rather shocking, counterintuitive profile of the successful, *blessed* individual.

Who is blessed?

He says those who mourn are blessed, for they receive comfort.

He says the meek are blessed, and those who are hungry and thirsty for righteousness; the merciful; the pure in heart; peacemakers; people who are mistreated for doing right. Those are "the blessed."

And finally, he says that people are blessed when they're insulted, persecuted, and lied about because of their pursuit of Jesus.

This list, this redefinition of success, has an order to it that is very important — especially the first thing Jesus mentions. He begins by saying, "Blessed are the poor in spirit, for theirs is the kingdom of heaven" (Matt. 5:3).

Blessed are the poor? I know some of you are thinking, Yes! I win! I am completely broke!

But Jesus isn't talking about money here. This isn't a reference to how much you either have or don't have. His words are "poor in spirit." Jesus is describing people who know they don't have it all figured out, people who are humble enough to ask for help.

This world's success puts the emphasis on being self-sufficient and self-reliant, acting as if we've got it all figured out. But Jesus redefines a successful life as one that humbly says to God, "I can't do this on my own. I need your help." From the world's perspective, that's the opposite of what successful people do.

So you've got to admit, it makes a pretty jarring contrast to our picture of winning business honors, moving into mansions, and being named *Time*'s Person of the Year. Jesus takes success and turns it upside down. We think that success is about being the king of the hill. Jesus points to the downtrodden, humble, and pure-hearted who refuse to play the world's game.

When our lives are defined by the world's definition of success, that's idolatry. So what's the *right* way to keep score?

There's a board game that has been around for a while called the Game of Life. If you've played that one, you know the object is to collect beautiful homes and expensive property. You win the Game of Life by landing the perfect job and driving the nicest vehicle.

My guess is that even if you never played *that* game, you're playing *the* game. And Jesus has a question for all game players. "What good will it be for someone to gain the whole world, yet forfeit their soul?" (Matt. 16:26). What's the point of the big promotion, the luxury car, and the second home if the price is your soul? Success would suddenly look like the deepest failure imaginable.

Maybe that's why we shouldn't be surprised when we read that as the rich young ruler walked away, he wasn't happy: "he went away sad, because he had great wealth" (Mark 10:22).

Taken out of context, that verse is almost funny. Why did he go away sad? Because he was rich! The way our minds are trained, it seems ludicrous, right? You don't go away sad because you're rich; you go away sad because you drive a seventeen-year-old three-cylinder Kia. Why would having so much make him sad?

Because he had too much to give up. He owned so much that it owned him. He was a rich young ruler, and Jesus was offering him an opportunity to be a poor young servant. But the god of success took his hand and led him away.

We don't even know his name. We have no clue what became of him. Chances are the rich young ruler went on to become the richer older ruler. My guess is that he went on to do pretty well playing the game of life.

But what if, instead of walking away sad, the man had said to Jesus, "Okay. I'll do it! I'll trade all that I have for all that you are." If he'd have said that, I imagine we'd know his name. Maybe there would have been thirteen disciples rather than twelve. Maybe there would have been five gospels rather than four.

Chuck's Decision

When Ann started talking about a church seminar, Chuck could only roll his eyes. "Let's go together," she said. "They're going to show us what the Bible has to say about money."

Chuck tried not to be condescending. "Honey, if I want financial training," he said, "I'll take a graduate level university course, not a Sunday school class."

But he saw the disappointment in her eyes. They'd been married for twenty-one years, but now there were tensions. Both of them felt it. Chuck finally came to her and said, "Okay. When does this thing start?"

Chuck had been a Christian since he was seven, but he realized he wasn't much of an expert on what was inside that big book. He'd heard plenty of sermons, but something happened at the seminar. Some of these verses actually *burned*.

For example, there was 2 Kings 17:33: "They worshiped the LORD, but they also served their own gods." That one all but reached out of the page and slapped him in the face.

Then there was Jesus in the New Testament saying, "You cannot serve both God and money" (Matt. 6:24). Both these verses had the word *serve*. It got Chuck thinking; he knew that God wanted more than lip service. He wanted living. He wanted action. For the first time, Chuck understood the spiritual picture that had defined Ann's world. And he called himself what he was: *idolater*. What an awful word, he thought. I've given over my life to serving the god of success.

He started to pray, but he felt helpless. He was in too deep with his life, his pursuit of significance. How could he ever get free?

One day he took his Bible into his closet, because that was

where Jesus had said to pray. Chuck wanted to be serious about this thing. And during that time, he felt God saying, "Give me your heart. That's what I want — but I want *all* of it."

And Chuck gave in. "I give it back to you," he prayed. "I repent from my idolatry. Just help me, Lord. I don't want to chase after money and success for another day."

In March of 2000, he visited New York City and one of the largest equity firms in the world. The firm wanted to partner with him. He came at it, he realized, much more humbly than he would have a few months earlier. He felt no self-importance, no arrogance — just an assurance that God was in charge and things would work out.

While he was there, history changed. The internet bubble burst; the NASDAQ plummeted. The crazy days of throwing money at the internet were over, just like that.

Chuck watched his own stock lose value by the day, and he wondered how he would have handled such a thing before that closet prayer. But you'll never guess how he felt experiencing that kind of loss. Are you ready for this? He felt rescued and renewed. The god of success lost whatever leverage was left for Chuck's heart. His heart was free to be fully God's.

Many of his business friends were absolutely devastated by similar losses. Chuck knew seven guys who committed suicide at some point. The primary reason: they were people who found their identity and purpose for living in their business performance, and when that went bad, life simply became unbearable. Chuck thought about them and thanked God one more time for coming after him.

Ann and the kids were glad to have him back. Whatever Chuck had lost when the bubble burst, he felt that God had more than replaced in things that really lasted. He decided he wanted to get into ministry, helping others deal with money. A friend advised against it. "Go talk to your wife," he said. "Tell her that these next years are prime earning years for a man. And ask her if she wants you to throw that away on ministry."

So Chuck and Ann had that talk. He passed on the man's question, and she passed another one right back. "Go back and talk to your friend," she said. "Ask him what years of his life he feels he should give to God."

Chuck smiled and took her hand. Together they committed their lives to serving God and following Jesus wherever he led and whatever it cost. These days Chuck is the CEO for Crown Financial Ministries and travels through the world teaching people what the Bible says about money and success.

Idol ID

What's your operating definition for success?
What goals, formal or informal, chart your course?

Everybody has an idea of what it would mean to have a successful life. Some of us are formal goal setters; others have more vague ideas about what direction we would like to head. How about you? What would have to happen for you to be successful? Where did you come up with your definition of success? Who set the standards?

Success is hearing Jesus say to you one day,
"Well done, good and faithful servant."
How will he measure your success?

We tend to measure it by tangible goals met. As a pastor, I'm sometimes tempted to define success by the numbers: how many people are coming to church. As an author I might be tempted to define success by how many books are sold. But I'm reminded that God measures success by faithfulness, by our obedience to the Scriptures. Compare and contrast the accepted measurement of success in the previous question with what the Bible teaches about success.

What drives your desire to be successful?
What is it that motivates you?

Remember, goals of advancement in the world are not necessarily sinful unless they become idols. You could have a goal, say, to own a restaurant of your own, simply because God has given you a passion for cooking. You could have a dream of playing professional basketball, owning your business, or any number of other things. The real question is, What drives your goals? What is your motivation? Is it for your glory or God's?

How often do you find yourself envying successful people?

Our culture spends a great deal of time spotlighting those who have made it to the top, based on the world's standards of success. Do you find yourself resentful or filled with envy? Is it hard for you to celebrate the success of others? Sometimes envy and resentment are leading indicators of our "pressure point" motives. If we feel driven toward certain goals, we're frustrated when others reach them first. How do you respond when others succeed?

CHOOSING JESUS:

Jesus My Purpose

*Idols are defeated not by being removed
but by being replaced.*

The god of success whispered to us, "Don't you want to be king of the hill?"

"Which hill?" we asked.

"Any of them. All of them." He smiled.

And we pursued a life of climbing, always climbing. Up hills. Up corporate ladders. Up lists. Up food chains. Up social registers. This god never had to make his case for what he was offering.

But along the way, climbing, working, earning, and achieving became ends in themselves. It was no longer about what we could do, but about whom we could out-do.

If we were honest we would have to say that it wasn't
for the Lord or even for others that we worked but for
ourselves.

And we had several unhappy surprises. One was that
we hurt people as we climbed over them or elbowed them
down the hill. Another was that we were always weary
from the effort. Not to mention always wary of challengers
to the throne. And the greatest surprise was that the top
of the hill wasn't nearly as great as we thought it would
be. The top of the hill ended up being a pretty lonely and
disappointing place. We wondered if maybe we had the
wrong hill.

And then we discovered one last hill. But this hill
already had a King, along with three crosses standing on it.
And he extends us a simple invitation: "Come and follow."
And as we follow him he turns success on its head. The first
will be last and the last will be first. The greatest among
you will be the servant of all. Consider others better than
yourself. To find your life you must lose it.

And so now, we still care about success, but we define
it very differently. He has become our purpose. We live for
serving him, for knowing him, for pleasing him. That's how
we define success.

the god
of money

In September of 2008, the worst finally happened: god died.

Who could have expected such a thing? He had seemed so immortal.

No one was taken more by surprise than his most fervent disciples. His health had never been stronger, and his influence was global.

In the wake of god's collapse, several of his most important and influential churches were abruptly shut down. Many of the faithful lost most of their religion overnight. They had depended on god for their future. What would they do now? The news of god's death brought weeping and wailing and gnashing of teeth all across the world. Governments tried to resuscitate him, hoping that he might show some signs of life.

Across the Sunday talk shows his death was analyzed: "How did we allow this to happen?" asked a typical moderator. "Why didn't we anticipate the collapse of our god?"

"It's not like it's the first time," a guest shrugged. "It goes in cycles. He'll come back, good as new. He always does."

"But this isn't like the past," countered another pundit. "The only time he was ever this bad off was back in the 1930s. I don't think he'll be the same for a long time."

The arguments went back and forth with a sense of urgency and hopelessness. They had put their hopes and dreams in god.

They had invested their time and energy in worshiping him. They counted on god to take care of them and keep them safe. Now, it seems, they had nowhere to run. God had seemed so powerful until now. He had provided better lives, bigger houses, and faster cars.

Do you remember when our god died? At least that's what it felt like to many when the economy seemed to be collapsing in 2008 and a recession seemed imminent.

The Almighty Dollar

The god of money has been around a long time. Back in the day, you knew him as gold or silver, and before that, heads of cattle or animal skins or anything that could be traded. These days he goes as cash, dough, bacon, benjamins, moolah, hundies, and the list goes on. He might take the form of a plastic card or be a file named "portfolio."

Before his health took a turn, the god of money had come into his own. He was riding high in the modern world. He's always been a god, but he hasn't always had this kind of power.

In the old days, you see, he was just your garden variety false god. Money was important, but the king had most of it. His palace was surrounded by teeming hordes of common people who had no wealth and no hope of ever getting any. They caught their fish or plowed their half acre or fought in the army. Rarely did they have two pennies to rub together, so they pursued more attainable gods.

Then the world began to change. Democracy created at least a somewhat more level playing field in the Western world. He was the star of the American dream, and when people talked about their "pursuit of happiness" the god of money would think to himself, What they really mean is the pursuit of me.

During the nineteenth century Horatio Alger popularized "rags to riches" stories. In these novels, some ordinary Joe worked his way from shoeshine boy to wealthy tycoon. This was the American dream — no matter who you were, you could hit it big. You could arrive at Ellis Island as a penniless immigrant and become the head of a business dynasty.

Money has grown so dominant in our culture that it's difficult for us to stand far enough back to get a perspective. No matter what we may say, many of us live as if the pursuit of wealth is the real goal in life. Sometimes we hear rich people say things like "money doesn't make you happy," but most of us think they all flew first class to some exotic destination where they got together and agreed to say that to make the rest of us feel better.

We pay lip service to the idea that money isn't that important, but how we spend our time and what we pursue seem to reveal our true belief. Money by the ton is the ultimate dream for so many people. When they talk about an ultimate fantasy, it's winning the lottery or inheriting a fortune from some rich relative. Mark Twain wrote, "Some men worship rank, some worship heroes, some worship power, some worship God, and over these ideals they dispute and cannot unite — but they all worship money."[19]

In Luke 12 Jesus is teaching a crowd of thousands. They are captivated as Jesus challenges his listeners to be faithful to God. "If you disown me here on earth," Jesus says, "I will disown you before my Father in heaven." Jesus is urging them to see this life through the lens of eternity. But there is a man in the crowd who isn't thinking about heaven; he's got money on his mind. Luke 12:13 reads, "Someone in the crowd said to him, 'Teacher, tell my brother to divide the inheritance with me.'"

It's likely that this was a younger brother asking this question. Perhaps he was bothered over the fact that according to the Levitical law, family inheritances gave two-thirds of the possessions to the older son and only one-third to the younger son. How you felt about the law was likely determined by whether or not you were the older or younger brother. Notice that he doesn't really ask Jesus a question about money; he comes to Jesus wanting him to back up what he already believes to be true about money and possessions. Sound familiar?

Jesus replied, "Man, who appointed me a judge or an arbiter between you?" Then he said to them (Jesus seems to turn his attention back to the crowd; he's going to use this as what my dad calls "a teachable moment"), "Watch out! Be on your guard against all kinds of greed; life does not consist in an abundance of possessions" (Luke 12:14–15).

Jesus makes the point that life is not about money and then goes on to tell a story about a man who made money and possessions his god. Of the thirty-eight parables Jesus tells, sixteen deal with the subject of money. Jesus seems to make it clear that the god of money is often God's main competition for our hearts. The problem isn't money. Money isn't the root of all kinds of evil, but the *love* of money is. Money is amoral. It's not good or bad in and of itself. But it holds the most potential to become for us a God substitute. When Jesus spoke on idolatry in the Sermon on the Mount, his only application was in the area of money. Matthew 6:24 reads, "No one can serve two masters. Either you will hate the one and love the other, or you will be devoted to the one and despise the other. You cannot serve both God and money." Money is consistently portrayed as God's chief competition. Like this man in Luke 12, we can all too easily make life about money and possessions.

The Parable of Frank

Frank Simmons was a man who was committed to doing whatever it took to be successful. He didn't come from a family with much money, but things were going to be different for him. Even when he was in high school he evaluated his future careers based on what would make him the most money. He considered going into medicine not because he was passionate about helping people but because he knew the money was good. But he finally decided on being a stockbroker. He got married his senior year in college and soon started a family, but he was working fourteen-hour days, often seven days a week. When he was at home he found he was preoccupied with work and the state of his investments. Then, when he started his own company, his occupation became his preoccupation. He became known as one of the best "market timers" in the business world. He always seemed to know what was about to take a downturn and what the next sure thing would be. His wife would ask if they could go out some time, just the two of them. She tried to remind him how quickly the kids were growing up; there were Little League games and dance recitals to attend. He would usually say something like, "Yeah, just let me get caught up. Next week should work." But he was always catching up, and before long they stopped asking. They knew where they stood. Frank would occasionally go to church to be seen by some of his clients, but most of the time his family would go without him.

By the time he was forty, Frank described himself as a self-made millionaire. But with the rise of the internet Frank realized that he could make some real money providing online investment opportunities. He would check his stocks twenty times a day and watch his fortune grow. One weekend he flew his wife to Naples to show her the beachfront property he was going to purchase for their dream home. He told her the big news: "By this time next year I'll take the company public. We'll be set for life. We'll have everything we could ever want. We'll be able to take life easy, eat, drink, and be merry. We'll have more than enough." She didn't say it out loud, but she thought to herself, For Frank, there will never be enough.

A few days later, back at the office, Frank closed on the property. That very night he was driving his Mercedes home from the office, and he took a corner a little too fast. By the time they found him, he had already been dead for hours. His death was big news in financial circles. He even made section B of the *Wall Street Journal* where they told his success story. They used words like *visionary* and *trendsetter* to describe him.

His life was the American dream. But while he was being remembered here on earth as a huge success, Frank was standing before his Creator trying to give an account of his life. And it turns out that with all of his entrepreneurial accomplishments and his extraordinary portfolio, God was not impressed. He was not impressed with the car he drove, his vacation home, or the company he had built.

John Tillotson puts it this way, "He who provides for this life but takes no care for eternity is wise for a moment, but a fool forever."

That's how the parable Jesus is going to tell might go if it were being told these days. But here's how Jesus told the story in Luke 12:16 – 19: "The ground of a certain rich man yielded an abundant harvest. He thought to himself, 'What shall I do? I have no place to store my crops.'" So this man is already rich and has more than he needs. Then he has a better than expected year. So what's this poor chap to do? He considers his options and reaches his conclusion: "This is what I'll do. I will tear down my barns and build bigger ones, and there I will store my surplus grain. And I'll say to myself, 'You have plenty of grain laid up for many years. Take life easy; eat, drink and be merry.'"

Mine

This story gives us a description of someone who is worshiping the god of money. If you look closely, you'll notice that the man refers to himself nine times in two verses. He speaks of *my* crops, *my* barns, *my* grain. Who gave him the good crops? Who gave him the ability to get rich? It doesn't seem to occur to him that he has what he has because God has given it to him. You don't have to teach this attitude toward our stuff. A two-year-old has a pretty limited vocabulary, but you can be sure he knows the word *mine*. Multiple times a day children grab something and say, "Mine." You put a bunch of two-year-olds in a room full of toys and it will sound like the "mine" birds on *Finding Nemo*. Mine. Mine. Mine. Mine. They are consumed with establishing ownership rights. You can watch an *angelic* looking child in the nursery as she gently brushes the hair of her doll and hums "Twinkle, Twinkle Little Star." But should another child come over and try to take her doll, she will unleash a fury of *The Exorcist* proportions. When we approach money from the perspective that it belongs to us, it just doesn't work. The key to keeping money in its right place is to remember that it all belongs to God. Whatever we have is on loan from God. Solomon reminds us in Ecclesiastes 5:15, "Everyone comes naked from their mother's womb, and as everyone comes, so they depart. They take nothing from their toil that they can carry in their hands." Psalm 24:1 simply puts it this way: "The earth is the LORD's, and everything in it." When we keep that perspective we understand our dependence on him and we worship him as the provider.

Imagine you haven't been on a vacation for a number of years. Finances are tight and it looks like this year will be another "staycation." But one day you get an email from an uncle that happens to have a beach house. He tells you you're welcome to stay in his beach house for a week. He turns over the key to you and says it's yours for the week. Now let's imagine you get to the beach house and you walk in and turn on the light, but the light bulb is burned out. You walk into the kitchen and there are no drinks in the fridge. At night the pillow is lumpy. And the beach isn't as close to the house as the picture made it seem. And so you fire off an email to your uncle laying out everything that is wrong and demanding to know what he is going to do to make it right.

In real life, you would never respond that way. For the week you are at the beach house you are constantly aware of and grateful for the generosity of your uncle.

In 2009 I had a revealing conversation with my dad, who was sixty-one at the time. That's near the age of retirement for most, although I don't think the thought has crossed his mind. He's always made a modest living but has been a disciplined saver. We were talking about his retirement account and I asked him what kind of hit he had taken. He said he was down about 40 percent from where he had been a year before. He's not alone, and I know many of you understand the implications of that. I asked him, "How are you and mom feeling about losing so much of your money?" He smiled at me and simply said, "Well, it was never mine to begin with." And then he quoted a Scripture from Philippians, "And my God will meet all your needs according to the riches of his glory in Christ Jesus" (4:19).

God has given us the use of his resources for a short time here on earth, and we have much to be grateful for. Go through your day sometime just recognizing that everything is God's. Get out of God's bed and walk into God's bathroom, and turn on God's shower, and then put on God's clothes. Eat God's cereal* and drink God's coffee. Get in God's car and head to work. When we start to see all of our resources as God's it helps us develop an attitude of gratitude that leads to a heart of worship.

Divine Attributes of Money

The reason money so often ends up being God's chief competition is that we tend to ascribe divine attributes to it. We look to money to do for us the very thing God wants to do for us. The man in Jesus' story does this as well.

---

*Frosted Flakes.

First he looks to money as his *source of security*. He tells himself that he has plenty of good things laid up for many years. We think if we could just save enough or accumulate enough we would have no more worries. Maybe you're afraid that the economy will collapse, or your health will fail, or there will be a terrorist attack, or you'll lose your job. And maybe you think if you could just save enough money, all your worries would go away. When we look to money as a security, it becomes our god, because that's where we are putting our hope and our dependence. Prayer becomes nice but not necessary because we have enough money to meet our own needs.

Maybe we should consider praying the prayer of Proverbs 30:8 – 9, which says, "Give me neither poverty nor riches, but give me only my daily bread. Otherwise, I may have too much and disown you and say, 'Who is the LORD?'"

The gods of power work from one shared premise: we can take care of ourselves. We can handle all our needs. The Lord is nice, but he really isn't necessary. We don't need to pray for our daily bread because we've got a pantry full of it. The gods of success appeal to our self-sufficiency.

Recently some close friends shared with us what happened in the first year of their marriage. The wife was the primary breadwinner and was finding her identity in money. She held it over her husband, and their marriage was falling apart. One day she bought two thousand shares of an IPO stock, costing a total of $180,000. It was everything she had, plus some. The stock opened up, and by the end of the day she had nothing left. In fact her family was now in debt to pay off her loss. She was devastated. She called her husband and he said, "It's just money. We still have each other." God began to teach her what really mattered. She learned that she had been dependent on herself and her own success. She saw herself as the provider, instead of being provided for by the Lord. She now sees that the day she lost $180,000 was one of the best days of her life. If that hadn't happened she wouldn't have realized her husband's love, and they likely would have divorced. Instead of being a committed mom, she would be continuing to find her worth in how much money she made. And most importantly she wouldn't have realized her dependence on God or put her complete trust in him. If money and success are your gods, may you be so blessed as to have them taken away from you, rather than spend your life bowing down to them only to find out you missed the real thing.

Second, the man in Jesus' story looks to money as his *source of satisfaction*. He thinks to himself, If I just accumulate a little more I can take life easy. Eat, drink, and be merry. Even before his good crop this man was wealthy, but he thinks that if he just had a little bit more, then he would be satisfied. But you have to wonder if things continued to go his way would his new barns be big enough, or would his happiness depend on getting even bigger barns?

My wife and I were young, newly married, and living in a tiny house that cost twenty-five thousand dollars. The monthly payment is etched into my memory, as numbers tend to be when you don't have much: $213 per month.

That seven-hundred-square-foot home was the best we could manage, and we looked on the bright side. For example, you just had to plug in the vacuum cleaner once; its cord could reach every wall in the house from one outlet. And we certainly didn't get tired running up flights of stairs or jogging over to "the west wing." It was small, but it was cozy.

We didn't have central heat; we had a floor furnace that took up most of the only hallway in the house. There wasn't room on the sides to walk around it, and it was too long to step over. So to avoid burning your feet, you had to take a running leap to clear it. Luckily, I had married a high school hurdler from the women's track team. I'd had no idea that skill would come in handy. I remember lying in bed in the morning and hearing her take a four-step running start to jump over the floor furnace.

The house did not have double-paned windows, so ice formed on the *inside* of our windows. It was my job to get the ice scraper from our car and scrape the ice off the windows inside the house. The walls were paper thin, so if the dog next door was barking or his stomach was growling, we got it in high fidelity. I'm fairly certain that the one bathroom we had was taken out of a small airplane.

We were full-time college students, and that was life. We ate our Ramen noodles and pasta three nights a week. A night on the town meant ice water for two and splitting an appetizer. Our goal was to keep the check under six bucks. Yep, the servers loved us.

My wife and I were recently lying in bed reminiscing and playing can-you-top-this with austerity stories, cracking each other up. Then we grew quiet and she said, "Are you any happier now than you were then?"

I didn't even have to think. "No," I said. "I'm not."

That story isn't unique; if you've been alive for a while, you can probably tell a similar one. But even though experientially we know that money won't satisfy us, we seem to always be chasing it. I know in my head that simplicity is highly underrated and wealth brings unanticipated complications, but something within my heart still says "more."

A 2006 study found that someone making $20,000 per year will indeed be happier than someone at the poverty level. After all, he isn't worried about his next meal or whether he'll continue to have shelter. But more money doesn't determine a person's level of happiness. Surprisingly, someone who makes $100,000 annually isn't much happier than the employee making $20,000. Huge difference in salary, but a minimal difference in happiness. As a matter of fact, the wealthier people are, the less time they spend pursuing enjoyable activities. The researchers concluded that "the belief that high income is associated with good mood is widespread but mostly illusory."[20]

Ecclesiastes 5:10 says, "If you love money, you will never be satisfied; if you long to be rich, you will never get all you want" (GN). The more money you have, the more you spend, right up to the limits of your income.

Most all of us have this appetite for money or possessions. And we think that if we could satisfy this appetite it would go away — if we could just make the money or buy the car — but that's not how it works. Instead, the more you feed it, the hungrier it gets.

Last, this man from Jesus' story looks to money as his *source of significance.* His focus is on himself and how much he has accumulated. He clearly found his identity in his stuff. We often do the same thing. We judge our worth by our net worth. When we ask, How much is a person worth? it seems clear that we're not just asking about their financial status.

THE COST OF A SMILE

Psychologists have studied what makes people happy. Not only do many of them find that money can't buy it; the opposite seems to hold true in many cases.

"Materialism is toxic for happiness," says University of Illinois psychologist Ed Diener. His research indicates that those who are less concerned about accumulating and spending are more likely to experience contentment.

University of Michigan psychologist Christopher Peterson indicates that forgiveness is the trait most strongly linked to happiness. Peterson has said, "It's the queen of all virtues, and probably the hardest to come by."[*]

[*] Marilyn Elias, "Psychologists Now Know What Makes People Happy," *USA Today*, December 10, 2002, *www.usatoday.com/news/health/2002-12-08-happy-main_x.htm*.

In his autobiography *Just As I Am*, Billy Graham recalls a story about meeting one of the richest men alive:

> Some years ago Ruth and I were on an island in the Caribbean. One of the wealthiest men in the world had asked us to come to his lavish home for lunch. He was 75 years old, and throughout the entire meal he seemed close to tears. "I am the most miserable man in the world," he finally said. "Out there is my yacht. I can go anywhere I want to. I have my private plane, my helicopters. I have everything I want to make my life happy, yet I am as miserable as hell." We talked to him and prayed with him, trying to point him to Christ, who alone gives lasting meaning to life.
>
> Then we went down the hill to a small cottage where we were staying. That afternoon the pastor of the local Baptist church came to call. He was an Englishman, and he too was 75 — a widower who spent most of his time taking care of his two invalid sisters. He was full of enthusiasm and love for Christ and others. "I don't have two pounds to my name," he said with a smile, "but I am the happiest man on this island."

Billy Graham relates how he asked his wife Ruth after they left, "Who do you think is the richer man?" She smiled. It was a rhetorical question because the answer was obvious.[21]

The god of money wants us to believe that our significance comes from what we make of ourselves. But we find our true identity in Christ. He has marked us as his own, and that's what makes us valuable. That's where our value is found. He forever determined our value when he died on the cross for us. But when we worship the god of money, a person's worth is determined not by the symbol of the cross, but by the symbol of a dollar sign.

The man in Luke 12 had put his trust in his money and possessions. His plan was to retire early and eat, drink, and be merry. But that's not what happened. Luke 12:20 records the end of the story,

"But God said to him, 'You fool! This very night your life will be demanded from you. Then who will get what you have prepared for yourself?'" The man died that very night, and his accumulation bought him nothing but a nicer funeral.

Is it possible that you have ascribed to money some of these divine attributes? Are you looking to money to do for you what God wants to do for you? Our currency in the United States has a slogan stamped right on its face that reads, "In God We Trust." That's more than a little ironic given the fact that so many of us have put our trust in money as god. It might be more helpful to put a question mark at the end of that statement written on our currency. So it would read like this: "In God We Trust?"

How we handle our money has a way of answering that question. Jesus put it this way in Matthew 6:21: "Where your treasure is, there your heart will be also." Where we put our money reveals what we've put our trust in.

Idol ID

How often do you compare what you have and how much you make to others?

The world teaches us to measure one another by payroll. The more we make, the more important we are. Therefore it's easy to find ourselves slipping into the lie that we are what we earn. And whether we truly, practically need more money or not, we chase after it for the affirmation it gives us.

Are you content with your salary? There are plenty of healthy reasons to be motivated toward greater earnings of course, but what are your reasons? Do you find yourself speculating on the salaries of coworkers or competitors?

Do you develop resentment when you feel you're worth more than you're paid?

If so, these are indications that money is becoming a god in your life.

How much anxiety do finances add to your life?

We've been through difficult economic times in recent years. Most of us have had financial worries, whether from the loss of retirement pensions, from unemployment, or from finding that there's too much month at the end of the money.

If you were to rank the things that cause you the greatest stress, where would you list money on that scale? How does it compare to such things as health, relationships, and job performance?

Maybe right now your financial situation is causing a lot of stress. Are you continually bringing that burden before the Lord? The apostle Paul talked about giving thanks in all circumstances. He said he learned the secret of being content in any and every situation, whether he was well fed or hungry. Can you give thanks and be content even in the midst of the financial challenges you are experiencing?

To what extent are your dreams and goals driven by money?

We've talked about personal dreams in this book, because they tell us a great deal about who we are and what makes us tick. What is your greatest dream, the thing that comes to your mind the quickest when someone asks, "If you had one wish ...?"

Do your dreams involve wealth and luxury? Winning the lottery? If so, why? Be honest with yourself as you reflect upon *why* you would want great sums of money. Would it be the freedom you would enjoy to pursue new goals with your time? Would it be the opportunities to give and to build new things? Or could it simply be the feeling of importance you would gain from being wealthy?

What is your attitude toward giving?

Think about occasions when you're called upon to offer a financial donation. This could be giving to church or Christian organizations. It could be a telephone solicitation or a contact from a charity you support. What emotions do you feel when you're asked to give? Are you annoyed? Do you find yourself wondering about the least amount you could acceptably give? Or do you find enjoyment and inspiration in using your finances to help others?

What percentage of your income do you currently give away? Deuteronomy 14:23 reads, "The purpose of tithing is to teach you to always put God first in your life" (LB).

I was talking to a friend of mine who is quite wealthy, but the only real indication of his wealth is his extreme generosity. He was recently talking to me about how easy it is for money to become an idol in his life. I asked him how he kept the god of money off the throne of his heart. Here's what he said: "Giving money away breaks its power. It's like you're saying to money, 'I don't even care about you. You are so unimportant to me that I can just give you away.'" He explains that when you give like that it destroys your idol of money because "it can't stand not being important."

If you want to find out how important money is to you, start giving it away.

Jesus My Provider

*Idols are defeated not by being removed
but by being replaced.*

The god of money was almost irresistible. He spun tales of sports cars, luxury homes, and all the good things he was going to buy for us. Yes, we had heard the old refrain that money can't buy happiness. We knew that. We had seen what it had done to people over and over.

But we were going to be different. We would know how to use the money without letting it use us. We didn't want to buy happiness; we just wanted to rent a little pleasure. But somewhere it all went wrong. Somehow the god of money became a slave driver.

He kept us running, following him, trying to keep him from getting away. We followed the green brick road until we longed to rest. We put our hope in what we might find at the end of the rainbow. We thought money would provide us with security, significance, and some measure of satisfaction. But strangely even when we had money we still felt broke.

Then we chose Jesus and discovered that he is our provider. He provides everything we need. He provides us with security because he never leaves us or forsakes us. He provides us with significance because our identity and value are found in his love. He provides us with satisfaction because our souls were made for him. We discovered that God would meet all our needs according to the riches of his glory in Christ Jesus.

the god
of achievement

Chuck Colson was born into a world of anxiety and fear, a nation mired in the Great Depression. His father taught him to appreciate the value of hard work and a dollar well earned. One of his earliest memories was of hungry people in a breadline and the awareness that there were people out there going hungry. But Chuck's father showed him what it took to survive; he worked hard all day, and then attended law school at night. Sunday afternoons were all the free time the old man had. On those wonderful days, the father sat on the back porch with his son and taught him the lessons:

- Always tell the truth.
- Give a good, hard day's work for a good day's pay.
- Take on any job, no matter how menial, and set your mind to the task.
- Work hard and you'll get ahead. This is the land of opportunity.

It was good old-fashioned Protestant work ethic, nothing complicated. But a generation of Americans believed those things, lived them, proved them. Chuck could have been their poster boy. He knew his life would be defined by hard work, by striving to get ahead until starvation, poverty, and shame weren't even in the rearview mirror. He would get a job, and he would do whatever it took to achieve.

Chuck's people hadn't attended college. He was the first, and he earned a scholarship to an Ivy League school. He excelled at everything, but his passion was politics. Chuck had his ideals. The opening to the Declaration of Independence moved him deeply — the idea that there were soldiers and sailors and marines who were ready to die for the idea of freedom.

So that's where he went next. He graduated with honors, got his law degree, and enlisted with the US Marines. The whole military world was exhilarating to him — pure grit and excellence, work ethic minus slackers. He was gung-ho and once again at the top of his class. He wouldn't settle for less.

One day, on maneuvers, he was instructed to lead fifty men on what seemed like an impossible assignment: take a high sand bluff. He got it done, based on pure determination. At the top, he thought, I'm a marine. I can do anything. And experience told him it was true. Chuck reached the rank of captain and ended up with an upper-level job in the Department of the Navy.

At twenty-nine, he ran a campaign for a Republican candidate for the US Senate and won by a huge margin. To get his man elected, he rolled up his sleeves and did things no one else was willing to do. He cut a few ethical corners here and there, played a dirty trick or two, but it was all about the result, right? And he was learning that politics was all about how far you were willing to go if you wanted to win. Whatever it takes to succeed.

He wanted to try his hand at the law, so he and a partner set up a law firm. They made good money. Yet his heart kept wandering over to the political world. He thought about Washington, the halls of power and the powerful. And he wanted to be there, to measure himself against the best. He had never yet found his limits. Chuck believed in the sheer power of the human will, in hard work, that if you pounded the wall enough times it would come down.

By 1969, at the age of thirty-seven, he landed in the White

House. He was invited to be one of an army of assistants to the president of the United States. Here he was, not even into middle age yet, advising the most powerful leader in the free world. Sure, he was a face in the crowd at first, but it wasn't long before the president was calling him in personally. He was an Oval Office fixture; he had risen to the tip of the top of the heap. He had worked hard. He had sacrificed, and achievement had come.

Chuck Colson wasn't just achieving; by almost anyone's standards he was overachieving. But there was still much that needed to be done. There wasn't anything he couldn't do. And now, at the right hand of Richard Nixon, he wondered if there was anything he *wouldn't* do.

Merit Badges

There is something within us that loves to *git-r-done.*

In the Western world, it's simply part of our DNA. Many of the first settlers of North America were very devout Christians who believed that God honors hard work and determined effort. The United States of America has been an experiment in freedom, an exercise in liberating people to go as far as their work will take them, and to prosper as well.

The problem is the danger of exchanging one king for another. If you've read this far, I would hope you agree that we're built to bow. We must find someone or something to serve. It's not surprising that, in our culture, personal achievement is a very powerful and alluring idol.

Think about our experience as children: Cub Scouts to Boy Scouts, Brownies to Girl Scouts. These are wonderful organizations, by the way, that teach any number of positive values — in particular, the value of achievement. You perform a task; you win a merit badge. Go on a hike and fulfill the given requirements, and you earn that colorful "camping" patch. Maybe you've been a scout or a member of a similar group. Do you remember how great it feels when the scoutmaster pins that patch to your uniform?

Or maybe in high school you got the letterman jacket for playing a sport, and every year you worked hard to add pins and patches to your jacket to show your achievements. Many kids, especially the high-achiever types, learn to find their identity and value in what they achieve. They put their hope in what they might one day be able to achieve.

And so the vest wrapped with badges, the jacket covered in patches, the trophies on the shelf, the ribbons, the medals, the report cards, the diplomas, the degrees, the promotions, the raises can become idols that we bow down to. They represent what we have accomplished through hard work and dedication. An idol could just as easily be a daily checklist that is completed or a kitchen that always stays clean or a perfectly manicured lawn. Obviously there is nothing wrong with any of these achievements; in fact, these achievements can be acts of worship that glorify God. But when our lives are all about getting things done, we can find that there is not much room for God. Instead, our approach to worshiping God can be checking off a box on our to-do list labeled "Go to church."

Making the Choice

In Luke 10 Jesus only has about six months left on earth. He knows he doesn't have much time left, and he knows what's coming. He spoke about the road to Jerusalem and what would transpire there. Jesus was certainly a high achiever. He needed only a few years of ministry to turn this world upside down. That's an impressive badge for him to iron on to his blue sash. He achieved more than anyone in history.

But Jesus wasn't preoccupied with a checklist of things to do and objectives to meet that day. He wasn't a slave to his schedule but simply stated that he did whatever the Father wanted him to do. He regularly took time to get away and pray. In the business of the day's itinerary the disciples may have thought Jesus didn't have time for the kids, that he had things to do and people to see, but Jesus said, "Let the little children come to me" (Matt. 19:14).

In Luke 10, even though he has lots to do and only a little time, it's surprising that Jesus took time to stop and visit with a few good friends, Mary and Martha. They're the two sisters of Lazarus, and Jesus clearly has a special relationship with that family. The Scriptures tell us that Martha opened her home to Jesus, and here's the scene that took place: two sisters, one hurrying around frantically with all the preparations, wanting to make the home worthy of Jesus, the other sitting quietly at his feet, listening.

> But Martha was distracted by all the preparations that had to be made. She came to him and asked, "Lord, don't you care that my sister has left me to do the work by myself? Tell her to help me!"
>
> "Martha, Martha," the Lord answered, "you are worried and upset about many things, but few things are needed — or indeed only one. Mary has chosen what is better, and it will not be taken away from her."
>
> — Luke 10:40 – 42

A lot of things are going on in those five sentences, but if we look at this story through the lens of idolatry there are two significant phrases:

- Martha was distracted.
- Mary had chosen.

The god of achievement distracts us from following Jesus by distracting us with all the things that need to be done. How often do we live with good intentions of spending time with Jesus and turning our heart toward him only to find at the end of the day that's the one thing on our checklist that we never got around to?

There are a few reasons why the god of achievement so often wins the daily battle for our hearts. The god of achievement offers a method of measurement. For many of us it's much easier to give our time to the tangible. We like to see what we got done. I can see that the house got cleaned, or the grass got mowed, or the contract got finished, or the budget got balanced, or the groceries got bought. When I get through spending time with Jesus, I don't see immediate results, but when I paint a room, the change is obvious. When I spend time in prayer and worship there isn't immediate visual evidence that I've accomplished something, but when I balance the budget, I've got something to show for it.

Martha was distracted by the preparations. This is the tyranny of the urgent. It's the list of things that need to be done right now. The most important marbles never seem to fit in the jar. Notice that what Martha was doing wasn't evil or sinful. In fact what she was doing was good because she was doing it for Jesus. But Jesus says that what Mary had chosen was better. What we are doing may be good, but the good is bad when there is something better.

Once again we see that many of the gods that battle for our hearts don't try to lure us with what is obviously wrong or overtly sinful. The issue of idolatry comes down to one word: choice. We've heard it from Moses. We've heard it from Joshua. We've heard it from Elijah. Now we hear it from Jesus. He commends Mary for the choice that she made.

A Little Competition

Martha demonstrates another characteristic of someone who struggles with the god of achievement. She compares herself and seems to be keeping score. Martha makes a point of how much more she has done than Mary. High achievers will turn almost anything into a competition. There are two related symptoms that indicate that the god of achievement has gained some ground in your life:

1. A constant frustration with people in your life who, from your perspective, aren't getting it done. Martha is frustrated with Mary that she isn't being a better teammate, but Mary doesn't even seem to realize she's competing in a game. This frustration with others for not doing their fair share comes to the surface in the form of criticism. Martha is critical of Mary's lack of productivity. Are you constantly critical of those around you for not getting enough done or not doing it well enough? Maybe you try not to be so critical but just get so frustrated you feel like you have to say something.

2. The second symptom is a constant sense of discontentment with yourself for not getting done what you hoped you would. Thomas J. DeLong, a Harvard Business School professor, describes his five hundred interviews with "high-need-for-achievement-professionals." More than four hundred of them "questioned their own success and brought up the name of at least one other peer who they felt had been more successful than they were."[22] What's interesting is that these professionals were selected from America's corporate leaders, yet they're making themselves miserable by constantly comparing themselves to others and feeling like they aren't achieving enough and are always running to catch up.

When we worship the god of achievement, getting things done and getting things done right becomes more important than almost anything or anyone else. In Psalm 46:10 the Lord reminds us to "be still, and know that I am God." It's hard to worship the god of achievement and be still and worship the Lord God at the same time. If it's difficult for you to take the time to be still and know that the Lord is God, that should be a warning sign. The rest of that verse in Psalm 46 goes on to say, "I will be exalted among the nations, I will be exalted in the earth." When we slow down long enough to know that the Lord is God, we are reminded of his sovereignty. He's got the whole world in his hands. Can I encourage you next time you find yourself being critical of others or especially hard on yourself to remember Mary and choose what is better? Take a deep breath. Be still. Know the Lord is God.

Hatchet Man

Chuck Colson had believed in God all his life. As a marine, he would stand on the deck of a ship in the quiet of the evening and enjoy the elegant scope of the evening canopy. It was easy to believe that someone had fashioned all this beauty and set these stars and galaxies in motion. But it must be someone just as distant, someone far too powerful and magnificent to worry about the little details of human life.

Chuck didn't feel he needed any cosmic input anyway. So far, he'd been pretty good at being his own god. He had been raised in a time when it was every man for himself, and you did what it took. Now, working in the White House, that meant trampling a few people who got in the way. But if you believed in the cause fervently enough, if you bought into the vision, then the end always justified the means.

Chuck had forged a tight relationship with an American president because of his loyalty and his willingness to do what was needed, no questions asked. By now, he was working almost exclusively in a gray area, the back channels of White House operation. His marching orders came from Nixon's mouth to his ear. And the power was intoxicating — he was given authority over all the communications that came out of the White House. He could pull a lot of strings, then shape the message.

In 1971, on his fortieth birthday, he received a strange gift. The *Wall Street Journal* profiled him on its front page with one of their signature line drawings. "Chuck Colson, the New Insider," it said. Underneath, the subtitle read, "White House Hatchet Man." There followed a journalistic piece about a man willing to do anything, no matter how much dirt got under his fingernails, a man sold out to the success of his master.

Hatchet man. If someone needed to be fired, send Chuck Colson, the former marine captain. "The man would walk through doors without opening them for me," said Nixon, who would hold up Colson as an example to his other aides. "Chuck is the one guy who can get things done around here," he said. "He doesn't let bureaucracy get in his way for a second. He goes out and he gets it done."

The *Wall Street Journal* hadn't talked to Colson for their interview. But they quoted others from his past. From deep in the guts of the article came a line that would take root and haunt him for a lifetime. Someone from the US Senate complimented his tenacity, his leadership and toughness, adding that Colson was "so tough he would run over his own grandmother."

At the time, the line didn't seem important, but it would be dredged up later when the name Charles Colson took on deeper significance. And for decades afterward, you'd see standard references to "Chuck Colson, who once boasted he'd run over his own grandmother" — though, of course, he had never said such a thing about himself. When I interviewed him for this book, he expressed his fear that the line would follow him to his tombstone.

As the 1972 presidential campaign began to take shape, Chuck Colson was one of the four or five men closest to Richard Nixon, and a key figure with the Committee to Reelect the President. It was destined to be a landslide victory over George McGovern, the Democratic nominee. Nixon had squeaked by Hubert Humphrey in 1968, but '72 was a laugher. Here was the president's national mandate, the affirmation he craved.

It was a great time to be in the halls of power. Even then, however, a couple of little-known reporters for the *Washington Post* were following up leads about an incident with some plumbers in a hotel. There had been a break-in, and rumors persisted that the connections led into the inner sanctum of the White House.

As the weeks and months passed, the stories began to move from deep in the paper to, eventually, the front page. The name of the hotel began to enter the public dialogue: Watergate.

And the time would come when these reporters, and many others, would start probing the man in the Oval Office as well as all the president's men who lurked in the background — including an assistant counsel named Charles Colson.

Choosing Better

Most of us resonate with Martha because we are a distracted culture. This is the ADD generation.* We're always on the move, always trying to get something done. Our phones are constantly dinging to let us know there is a text we need to return or an appointment we're going to be late for.

Martha had Jesus right there in her presence, and she was setting up a situation about which her grandchildren might someday ask, "What was it like? Jesus in your home! That must have been amazing. What did he say? What was it like to be with him?" And she'd have to say, "Well, to tell the truth, there was this special china I was trying to find. It had been in our family for a long time, and I just had to have that for dinner with Jesus. So I never really heard what he said. I just caught bits and pieces of the conversation as I flew through the room. Your Great-Aunt Mary will have to fill you in."

How many times have we been so distracted that we've missed a divine moment? How many things does God long to say to us, but he keeps getting our voicemail because we're too busy to pick up? It's idolatry of a dangerous sort, because it's shot through with

---

*Squirrel.

virtue and traditional values. Work hard. Don't be like that loafer, Mary! Who's going to get this stuff done?

I wonder how important that stuff was to Martha after her friend had been crucified, resurrected, and taken up into heaven. I wonder what she would have given for just a few moments to sit at his feet.

"Mary has chosen what is better."

That's a choice we can make every single day when we choose to make our relationship with God more important than anything else on the calendar or to-do list. I know I've already said this, but I want to be clear. Working hard and achieving goals are an important part of a God-glorifying life. But they are *not* life. They are not even a measuring stick for the worth of life. When we give them our soul, they become one more false god — a great cluster of merit badges, melted into a golden calf. Remember, the people had asked for "gods who will go before us" (Ex. 32:1). That's what we want our achievements to do, to pave the way as we move through life.

And when Aaron's group had made the idol, they said, "These are your gods, Israel, who brought you up out of Egypt" (Ex. 32:4). It seems crazy. How could they make something, then give it credit for where they had come?

But that's the illusion of achievement. We begin to believe in what we've done, but it's more than that. What we've done begins to define who we are. We are our achievements. When you meet other adults these days, they introduce themselves with name and business. "Hi, I'm Kyle. I'm a pastor." "Hi, I'm Judy. I'm an interior designer." I know that's just how we talk, but our jobs are becoming almost hyphenated to our names, which of course is how surnames began. John the miller became John Miller; Peter the baker became Peter Baker.

I read a story about Sheila Walsh, the singer who was once the cohost of the *700 Club* on television. She experienced an emotional crisis in 1992, in the midst of her great success. One morning she was in front of the cameras, and the same night she found herself in a psychiatric hospital. The doctor asked her, "Who are you?"

She said, "I'm the cohost of the *700 Club*."

He told her that wasn't really what he meant, so she identified herself as a writer and singer.

The psychiatrist said, "But who are you?"

She sighed and answered, "I don't have a clue." And he told her that's why she was there.

"I measured myself by what other people thought of me," Sheila writes. "That was slowly killing me. Before I entered the hospital, some of the *700 Club* staff said to me, 'Don't do this. You will never regain any kind of platform. If people know you were in a mental institution and on medication, it's over.'"

She didn't think that was a big deal, because it seemed to her that she had already lost everything. And sometimes, that's what it takes for us to connect with God. The idols have to be burned down, and that can be incredibly painful. We have to let go of a lot of garbage before we can gain the one thing worth having — but we're very attached to that garbage. It seems like part of us.

Music always spoke to Sheila Walsh, and it's not surprising that God reached her through song lyrics. At her worst moment of crisis, she found a little church on the streets of Washington, DC, and went there to quietly worship and reconnect with God. As she did so, she remembered an old hymn that said, "Nothing in my hands I bring. Simply to thy cross I cling."[23] God doesn't want our résumés; he wants *us*. It takes a lot of faith to let go of all that junk and take hold of the cross with both hands.

Welcome to the Machine

Toward the end of his life, Chuck understood that life is made of choices. He would advise young people, "Just stop occasionally.

Take stock of who you are and what you're doing. I never did that. I was too busy."

From the distance of the years, he realized he had gone so far and enjoyed it too little. Who had time to enjoy? The work was sacred. You worked, and that created more work. It never ended. Chuck's kids were growing up, and he never had enough time for them. His soul belonged to the reelection of the president, who had offered him a cabinet position or whatever he wanted in the second term — anything to keep him doing the things he was doing.

Every now and then, he would hear his peers talk about the DC social circle, about extracurricular stuff, and he would realize there was none of that in his family's life. Who am I? he would think during those moments. What's all this for? Where does it lead? But the big question was always, What's next? It always had been a pressing question for him: school, college, military, law, politics — what worlds to conquer next? He was forty-one now, and he'd put his stamp on American history. But he wondered what would happen when he hit the ceiling, when he knew he could go no farther. There was a hollowness inside him; he couldn't ignore it. Maybe, he thought, he was just tired, burned out. But he found himself asking questions that had never occurred to him.

America had never seen anything like the Watergate scandal. It was as if the country shut down for several months while the hearings droned on, the reporters dug up dirt, and the president, a man as driven and achievement-based as Chuck Colson, felt it all slip through his fingers — everything he had worked for throughout his entire life. Two years after a landslide election victory, he was facing a stark decision between impeachment and resignation.

Chuck was caught up in the tide of national anger. All he knew to do was go back into law. In the midst of the crisis, he went to see an old friend and client, Tom Phillips, president of Raytheon Company. Chuck respected Tom, a guy from his generation who shared his work ethic. He was a little surprised to see how calm and composed Tom was on this day, however; the man's desk was actually clean. There were rumors that Tom had experienced some kind of religious thing. Chuck asked him what was up.

His friend was a little reticent. He looked away and said, "I've found Jesus. My life belongs to him now."

Where Chuck came from, that was crazy talk. You might occasionally go to church, but you didn't talk about "finding" Jesus or committing your whole life to him. Not in the Northeast.

Then again, Chuck had been humbled; he was being summoned and questioned by grand juries. His name was being trashed in the national media. The calmness of his friend was a thing of wonder. A little later, he called Tom and asked for another visit. "I want to hear more about this religious thing that's happened to you," he said.

The two of them sat on a porch, and Tom talked about going to a Billy Graham crusade. He pulled out a little book, *Mere Christianity* by C. S. Lewis, and read aloud about what Lewis called "The Great Sin," pride. The writing was sharp and intellectual, and the ideas turned Chuck inside out. He had been raised to think of pride as the prince of values: pride of work and of name, pride of accomplishment. But now he could see that it carried with it a dark side. Pride could drive you too hard for your own good. It could make you arrogant and contemptuous of others.

This book is about me, Chuck thought. This is where I've been. He felt naked and helpless before its declarations. The courts could charge him with nothing more painful than this. The hatchet man had been disarmed.

Tom wanted to pray with him, to invite Chuck to a new life. Chuck wasn't ready for that, but he agreed to take the C. S. Lewis book home and read it. On his drive, he cried out to God. His anxiety was so deep that he worried about wrecking the automobile. Chuck pulled to the side of the road and sat thinking, talking to a God he'd never had time for in the past. And there came an amazing feeling that God was listening. This kind of thing had never been part of Chuck's experience. He was a solid, real-world kind of guy. Had he gone around the bend?

The next morning, he figured, it would all blow over. He'd be in his right mind again. Instead, he felt excitement about the new ideas — and peace, *real* peace, tremendous release from the awful burden of being Chuck Colson, the overachiever, the master of all he surveyed.

He could see his sin and weakness now, and strangely enough, that was relieving. It wasn't all up to him anymore, because he could lay everything at the feet of God.

He dived into Lewis's book — read, reread, underlined, reflected. It sealed the deal. From that day onward, his life belonged to Christ. But what to do about the legal issues? Chuck thought about this and found a charge he could agree he was guilty of. He offered the guilty plea and served his time in prison. Not surprisingly, the media found out about his conversion, and the derision turned to ridicule. Surely it was all a ploy, declared the pundits.

It didn't matter. With all the public turmoil, Chuck Colson knew he was a new human being. All the power of his old idols had been stripped away, and he knew what the true source of power was. Strange, he would think, as they led him to his cell. Strange how a man can go behind bars, yet be more free than he's ever been.

Blown Away

Achievements are good things until they become our gods. They can help make this world a better place. But in the end, we can't put our faith in them because they shrivel like all the stuff of the world, and they are blown away. That's why Paul wrote in 2 Corinthians 4:18, "So we fix our eyes not on what is seen, but on what is unseen, since what is seen is temporary, but what is unseen is eternal."

A few years ago, a group of senior citizens, all at least ninety-five years old, were asked this question: "If you had life to live all over again, what would you do differently?"

They weren't given multiple-choice answers but allowed to say whatever they were thinking. The responses varied, of course, but the three themes that dominated the replies were as follows:

1. If I had life to live all over again, I would reflect more.
2. If I had life to live all over again, I would risk more.
3. If I had life to live all over again, I would do more things that would live on after I am dead.[24]

I believe there's deep wisdom to be gained from the observations of this world's experienced sojourners. What they're saying to us here is, I wish I had slowed down a little. I wish I hadn't always played it safe, but had really gone for it occasionally. And I wish I had invested myself not in these rusty merit badges, but in eternal realities.

If you're an achievement addict, consider this your wake-up call. Stop to reflect, to think about who you are and who you will be when all the earthly accomplishments have dried up and blown away. Consider the words of Jesus to Martha and the hard-learned lesson from Chuck Colson, and don't just choose what is good; choose what is better.

A New Resume

For an overachiever, hard-driven by accomplishment, going to prison is like stripping a junkie of his narcotics. Chuck Colson had to learn to do nothing. He thought of his father's teachings again: take on any task, no matter how menial. Well, he'd gone from practicing law to prison laundry.

But he was also writing. He found himself counseling other prisoners. What a fresh experience that was, just helping men who couldn't read or write. He came to realize that what he really liked was serving others. The old ideals hadn't changed. He still believed in America, and in working to make it better. But this time he wasn't working hard for the sake of achievement and self-advancement. This time the hard work was an act of worship for the glory of God.

Even so, from the world's perspective, he had no future, not after public shame and imprisonment. He didn't understand that God has his own plans and timetables. He was the second-to-last Watergate figure to leave prison, and he couldn't have known that the best was yet to come for him. He founded Prison Fellowship, which has had an enormous impact on American incarceration. He published many books and touched millions of lives through a daily radio show and countless others simply through the power of his story.

When he passed away in 2012, the memorial procession passed the Watergate complex on the way to the National Cathedral. No one quoted the "grandmother" line. There wasn't a lot of talk about politics. Instead, it was all about a loving father and patient grandfather to an autistic child, about a man who defended the weak, embraced sinners, and spoke the truth.

They quoted Abraham Kuyper, one of Chuck's heroes, who said, "There is not one square inch in the whole domain of our human existence over which Christ, who is Sovereign over all, does not cry: 'Mine, that belongs to me!'"

Chuck, who had thrown over his own idols, loved that quote, because he understood that life was not ultimately defined by what he had done, but by who he belonged to.

Idol ID

How has your life up to now been defined by achievement?

Think back to your childhood. How much was it ingrained in you that you needed to be highly productive, whether in schoolwork or other activities? In what area did you want to achieve?

Once again, these are all positive factors in growing up. Achievement is good, but sometimes we get the idea that what we achieve is who we are, or that it determines our value and justifies our existence.

How do you define your identity to others? To yourself?

Most of us begin with our name and proceed to our occupation when introducing ourselves to others. It makes sense: we're identifying how we spend a great amount of our time and what our important skills are. But to what extent do we consider our work as defining us? Are you your job? Is work the great driving force in your life?

Why do you do what you do?

Think through what you're currently working hard to achieve. Hard work is good but why are you doing it? Is it to prove yourself? Is it because of your competitive drive to be the best? Or are you working hard for the glory of God?

When do you feel the most guilty or self-critical?

Does a lack of productivity—even for a mere day or a couple of hours—bring you frustration and cause you to feel bad about yourself?

Gordon MacDonald, in his classic book *Ordering Your Private World*, talks about the difference between being *driven* or *called*. Driven people are highly busy, and they see that as a sign of their success or significance. They don't tend to enjoy their work, but only the results of it, the fact of reaching the goal. Guilt is a motivation factor in all they do.

Those who are called are people who have learned to feel the freedom of being in the will of God, whom they can experience in the whole process and not simply the results. They are less competitive than others, and they can give themselves permission to fail. The irony is in the end this freedom to fail often results in greater accomplishments.

Work and achievements are blessed by God, and have been since Adam and Eve received their work assignments in the garden. But they are ways of feeling the joy of serving God. Once they become something else, they can be toxic.

part 4

the temple
of love

the god
of romance

Every neighborhood has a tomboy. When the guys get together to play some ball, they're usually not surprised if one of the guys is, well, a gal. It's classic playground tradition.

Except that everyone figures the tomboy will grow up to be another traditional figure, the "girl next door."

Shannon showed no signs of that direction. A tomboy since childhood, she continued to push the masculine side of her personality to the forefront. She came to think of herself as a living, walking mistake. When God made her, she figured, he'd poured a boy spirit into a girl body. Such a mindset is going to lead, sooner or later, to frustration and despair.

There were reasons. Shannon had been a victim of sexual abuse. That experience damages different people in different ways. For Shannon, it was an indication that being a girl placed her in danger; being pretty or feminine enhanced her as a target. Things were done to girls. If she wasn't a girl, maybe they'd leave her alone.

Shannon also came out of her abuse with a distorted view of relationships with the opposite sex. Though she hung out with guys and participated in sandlot games with them, she had no clue how to relate to them outside of athletics.

Most of all, she believed that she had no real value as a human being. Otherwise, why would anyone have done that thing to her?

The abuser was a male figure who was supposed to be a figure of trust. So who or what in life could be counted on? The question seemed rhetorical, because there was no apparent answer.

Shannon's only response was to toughen up. She wore her hair short, focused on sports, and stayed grimy and sweaty as much as possible. It matched the dirtiness she felt on the inside. She was sarcastic and assertive, but it was only a mask to hide the depression and confusion beneath the facade.

All of this was relatively manageable until she hit puberty. Before that, Shannon could simply be a little girl climbing trees, stealing second, playing catch. But adolescence was approaching, and things were starting to change. The girls painted their nails and talked about clothing; she didn't fit into that world at all. And the dynamic was changing with the guys too; it wasn't going to be cool to be a tomboy much longer, as they began to relate to girls through attraction rather than athleticism.

Shannon had no place at all. I'm a mistake, a misfit, she thought. I have no future.

As she thought about it, she realized that she craved love — to give it and to receive it. Love could rescue her from shame; it could make her feel like a person of worth. Like many adolescents, she sexualized the feelings in her heart. So desperate was her desire for caring that she reached back to the time of her abuse, and she took hold of the idea of sexual expression she found there. It was the most obvious way to get attention, to find some form of love.

It was unhealthy; it was self-destructive. But it was all she knew. She understood the deal. I will consent to *this*, let you do *that*, and you will give me love and acceptance in return. But of course, no real, satisfying connections came out of that arrangement. She offered sexuality, and that's all she got back. Throwing herself at boys didn't make her feel any more complete as a girl. She coveted love and acceptance from her own gender. Almost inevitably, she began to wonder about a lesbian identity. She pursued the question not overtly, but through pornography.

Again, she was exploring the question through sexualizing it. This hadn't helped her understand boys, and it didn't help her understand girls. Once again her pursuit of love didn't bring her any sense of acceptance or belonging. In fact the harder she chased it the lonelier she felt. She just wanted to love and to be loved. Shannon was coming on to guys sexually, yet consuming same-sex pornography privately, trying desperately to satisfy the hunger in her heart for intimacy, but instead she felt a growing sense of isolation.

The Myth of Hearts and Flowers and Meatloaf

Our culture holds up romantic love as the greatest and noblest of pursuits. We are led to believe that the need for romantic affection is built into every single one of us, so that we instinctively yearn for that tingly, bubbly feeling that we call "falling in love." We spend our lives in hopes of finding our soul mate — that one person out there just for us.*

The message to those who aren't married or at least dating someone is that you won't be content or complete unless you're in a relationship. It starts early. When my middle daughter was four years old she watched a Disney movie about a prince and princess living happily ever after. When it was over, she asked me, "Daddy, who am I going to marry?" I told her that she didn't need to worry about that right now and that I would make that decision when the time came. But the not-so-subtle message that she picked up on is that "if you don't have a prince, then you can't be a princess."

---

*Since there are more women than men on the planet statistically this is impossible. Besides if there was such a thing as a "soul mate" it would only take one person getting it wrong to ruin it for the rest of us. Just sayin'.

Even at church sometimes a single person gets the impression that they are somehow incomplete. I was looking in a Christian bookstore under the section for single adults. There were about twenty different titles. Seventeen of them dealt with finding your future mate. My favorite title was *If Men Are Like Buses, How Can I Catch One?* And well-meaning people say things like, "If you want to find someone wonderful, you have to be someone wonderful." In other words if you're not with someone, there must be something wrong with you.

For many, romantic love becomes the focus of their lives. Our popular culture tells us that love makes the world go round and that all you need is love. Pick your cliché, but what seems clear is that romantic love is the most important subject we have. Nearly

THE ULTIMATE NARCOTIC

Limerence. Psychologist Dorothy Tennov coined the term *limerence* in the 1970s. It refers to the phenomenon of falling madly, passionately in love, including what happens chemically in the body. Have you ever been "lovesick"?

Tennov interviewed five hundred people about the love in their life. Limerence describes a powerful emotional attachment that comes over a person who is powerfully attracted to some other person.

It's an overpowering infatuation that involves "intrusive thinking" (not being able to concentrate on any subject but the object of our love); "putting the other on a pedestal"; agonizing over whether the feelings are reciprocated; fear of rejection; and some physical effects such as heart palpitations, loss of appetite, and paralyzing shyness around the object of affection.

Dopamine, the body's pleasure chemical, surges during

all of our music is about this kind of love, and it's been that way for a long time. You know those Harlequin romances? Five and a half of those novels are sold every second.[25]

The Beatles tell us that all we need is love. Burt Bacharach asserts that what the world needs now is love, sweet love. Another old classic tells us that love makes the world go round. Robert Palmer might as well face it, he's addicted to love.

The singer Meatloaf assures us that he'd do anything for love. In fact Meatloaf would run right into hell and back. Yet I'm always puzzled by that one, because later in the song, he says that though he'd do *anything* for love, he won't do "that." I always wondered what "that" refers to. Where is he drawing the line here? He won't share the remote? Won't put down the toilet lid? Won't get rid of

limerence, so that love has a kind of stimulant effect. Energy is increased; appetite decreased. It's a blissful feeling, but a two-edged sword; rejection can cause a dangerous crash. The increase in dopamine can bring about a decrease in serotonin, a chemical that helps us make wise decisions. This helps to explain why people who are "head over heels" will do crazy, spontaneous things they would never ordinarily do.

Those who study limerence say that it burns itself out after eighteen to thirty-six months. At that point, if things have worked out for the couple, and the love is returned, then a deeper, more comfortable and less disruptive stage of love will result. The honeymoon, as they say, is over, but the marriage can begin.*

Limerence is a fairly new field of study, but it certainly offers its share of explanations for the sometimes wonderful, sometimes insane experience of romantic love.

* Frank Tallis, "Crazy for You," *The Psychologist* 18, no. 2 (February 2005): 72–74.

that unibrow? Did she want him to change his name? That seems like a reasonable request from a potential Mrs. Meatloaf.

But the song raises a good question. Would you do anything for love?

If so, then romantic love has officially reached god status in your life.

Here's a surprising thought: life was never meant to be all about romantic love. Much of what we think of as romantic love was actually an invention of Western culture, something that didn't take hold until the Middle Ages. C. S. Lewis, one of the world's greatest classical scholars, wrote a study called *The Allegory of Love.* In it he shows how troubadours during medieval times popularized this hearts-and-flowers conception of love between a man and a woman. And it simply took hold of our part of the world. As a matter of fact, he wrote that he believes that this development had a greater impact than the Protestant Reformation! It caused us to believe that the great purpose of life is the pursuit of an emotional, dramatic, passionate, romantic love.[26]

It's not as if romantic affection itself didn't exist before that; go read the Song of Songs in your Bible if you doubt that it did. But romantic love as the great quest, an obsession, something we must have or be miserable, is a human, cultural invention. God has wired most of us for intimate fellowship, for a special mate, someone to complement us. But in modern times we've inflated that idea to crazy proportions. We look to romantic love as the secret to our satisfaction and the missing piece to make life feel complete.

Rodgers and Hammerstein wrote a song called "Falling in Love with Love," and they were onto something with that idea. It's love itself that becomes so attractive, once we've seen the cowboy ride into the sunset with the girl, or Harry meet Sally, or Romeo come to Juliet's window. We want the hearts and the flowers, and we want our stories to end with the words "and they lived happily ever after."

Romantic love is a good thing, but when we make it essential to life then it becomes a false god. When we put our hope in romantic love and sacrifice so much for it, you have to ask if this beautiful gift from God has actually replaced him. When that happens the ending is rarely "happily ever after."

Looking for Love

In Genesis 29 we come to a love story that reads more like something from a reality TV show than from the first chapters of the Bible. It's *The Bachelor BC.*

Jacob, Abraham's grandson, has left home and has gone to visit a relative named Laban. When he gets there he seems to almost immediately fall in love with Laban's daughter Rachel. "Now Laban had two daughters; the name of the older was Leah, and the name of the younger was Rachel. Leah had weak eyes, but Rachel had a lovely figure and was beautiful. Jacob was in love with Rachel and said, 'I'll work for you seven years in return for your younger daughter Rachel'" (Gen. 29:16 – 18).

Jacob was in love? What did he really know about Rachel at this point? Mostly that she had a lovely figure and was beautiful. But he had it bad for her and makes a deal with her father that he'll work seven years for her hand in marriage. That's a significant sacrifice he's willing to lay down on the altar of romantic love. But my guess is that most of you have done some crazy things in the name of love. Most of us have sacrificed significantly for love.

When my wife and I were dating I took her to see a show called *Stars on Ice.* She enjoys watching ice-skating. She loves the costumes, the music, the graceful movement. I remember sitting there watching the skaters come out in their little outfits and dance around on the ice. I hated every second of it. I knew I would but I still bought the tickets and made time in my schedule to take her. We've been married now for seventeen years and my wife knows that the only way we're going to watch people skate on ice is if they're wearing pads and carrying large sticks, and there are goals at the ends of the rink.

As much as I hate to admit it, that's not the truth. My wife would only need to bat her eyes at me and I would be more than happy to give up some money and time to take her to see an ice-skating show. Why? Because I would do anything for love, even that.*

What we sacrifice the most for has the most potential to become a God replacement. Of course, the key to honoring God is not to love our spouses less sacrificially. In fact in Ephesians Paul challenges husbands to love their wives as Christ loved the church and gave himself up for her (Eph. 5:25).

Jacob loves Rachel but doesn't have any real romantic interest in Leah. Leah is described as having "weak" eyes. That doesn't mean that she couldn't see well or required thick horn-rimmed glasses. It contrasts Leah's appearance with that of her sister. It's possible that having "weak" eyes is meant to be a compliment. But if you have a friend who is setting you up with a girl and you ask "What does she look like?" you know you're in trouble if the answer is, "Well, she has nice eyes."

Jacob works for seven years to get Rachel as his wife and in Genesis 29:20 we read an incredibly romantic verse, "So Jacob served seven years to get Rachel, but they seemed like only a few days to him because of his love for her." That is so sweet. In the next verse Jacob says to Laban, "Give me my wife. My time is completed, and I want to make love to her" (v. 21).

Okay. That's not quite as sweet. Probably wouldn't find that verse in a Hallmark card. But seven years is a long time to wait.

To make a long story short, they hold a feast. Laban probably

---

*And she has a lovely figure and is beautiful. (This footnote was added after she read the first draft of the book. Please don't tell her I added this. But if you decide to tell her I added this please don't tell her I told you not to tell her.)

plies his new son-in-law with wine. Jacob stumbles to his tent, and they send in his wife, according to tradition, for the marriage to be consummated. But the next morning he wakes up, rolls over, and opens his eyes, and a pair of weak eyes are staring back at him. He thought he was marrying Rachel but somehow ended up marrying Leah.

I know what you're thinking: How did that happen? I'm not sure, but my guess is he was really drunk and it was really dark and he didn't realize it was Leah until the light of day. It sounds like a bad Jerry Springer show.

Jacob sobers up quick and stumbles into his pants as he runs out of the tent looking for his father-in-law. He's no doubt furious. Laban seeks to renegotiate the deal and tells Jacob that he can have Rachel as his wife as well but it will cost him another seven years of labor. Jacob has no choice but to go along with the new deal. Now he has two wives and one big mess. But it's not Jacob I really feel sorry for in this story; it's Leah. Leah really loves her husband. She would do anything for him to love her back. She undoubtedly feels incomplete without her husband's love and affection.

You Complete Me ... Kind Of

The other day I came across a website that listed the top ten romantic lines from the movies. You'd probably recognize most of them. The number one line, according to this list, was from the movie *Jerry Maguire*, starring Tom Cruise. You might remember that moment when Tom Cruise turns to Renée Zellweger and with tear-filled eyes and quivering lip says, "You. Complete. Me." The whole movie has been building up to that one line. What Jerry Maguire couldn't find in success at work or in casual hookups he finally finds in romantic love.

But the truth is, if there were a *Jerry Maguire 2* — and I'm not suggesting that there should be — you would find that she didn't complete him anymore and he didn't end up completing her. It felt that way initially; the rush of passion and emotion felt like completion. But it wouldn't have lasted. And chances are the sequel would find the main characters moving on to someone else in hopes of being completed.

What happens, however, when we believe ourselves to be incomplete without a mate? We begin a relentless search. Everything is put on hold. Nothing "counts" until we find that partner who is supposed to be at our side. I have a single friend in his late twenties who bought a house a few years ago. When I went over to visit I commented on the fact that he had absolutely no furniture in the house except for a mattress on the floor and card table set up in the kitchen. He explained to me that he decided not to buy any furniture because when he got married his wife would want to pick everything out. Umm ... he wasn't even dating someone at the time. He had an imaginary girlfriend to match his imaginary furniture. Two years later he's still got things on hold waiting to meet that special someone and for life to really begin.

When we look to someone other than God to complete us and define our lives, it's idolatry. It's also futile because God is the only one who can complete us. We are made for him. A relationship with a life partner is a wonderful and precious gift, but it was never meant to replace a relationship with the giver.

Spoiler alert: when you make a relationship with someone else your god, it will eventually be marked with disappointment and bitterness. When you look to someone to be your god, they are going to let you down. When you say to someone, "I want you to satisfy me; I want you to save me; I want you to be my source of significance," what you're really saying is, "I want you to be god to me." Well, that's a lot to ask of someone. That puts a lot of pressure on the relationship, and given enough time that pressure will cause some cracks.

Like all idols, the god of romantic love promises big and pays off in pain. The adrenaline rush of new love isn't built to last. It passes. The honeymoon ends.

The truth is, you and I were made for a love far deeper, far richer than what any human relationship can offer.

A New Love

Over the years it's Leah, not Rachel, who gives her husband plenty of children. If you read through the names of her children they tell the story of the disappointment and heartache she is experiencing in her love life.

Leah names her first son Reuben, for "the LORD has seen my misery. Surely my husband will love me now" (Gen. 29:32).

She has a second son and says, "Because the LORD heard that I am not loved, he gave me this one too" (v. 33).

With the third son, she says, "Now at last my husband will become attached to me, because I have borne him three sons" (v. 34).

With each son she has, Leah thinks maybe now her husband will love her. Maybe now he will be attached to her. But with each child she is left disappointed. For years Leah puts her hope in romantic love, but she continues to feel the pain of rejection and loneliness.

But then, in verse 35, there is a compelling twist. "She conceived again, and when she gave birth to a son she said, 'This time I will praise the LORD.' So she named him Judah. Then she stopped having children" (Gen. 29:35).

"This time I will praise the Lord." Leah is taking her husband off the throne of her heart and giving God his seat. This time she puts her hope not in her husband, but in the Lord. How many times has the god of love left you brokenhearted? Maybe this time you should praise the Lord.

The name she chooses, *Judah*, is a play on the Hebrew word for *praise*. And if we turn to the beginning of the New Testament, the gospel of Matthew, we see the family tree of Jesus. Here's what we read when the genealogy gets to this branch: Jacob was the father of Judah. It's not Jacob's son Joseph nor Benjamin, his two favorites by Rachel, that are referenced. Instead it's Judah, the fourth son of a hand-me-down wife. Judah, the commemoration of a moment when a woman turned her eyes back to God.

Like Leah, most of us have learned that when we experience rejection from someone that we care about and love, it can be painful.

A friend of mine was recently giving me some frequently used breakup lines and describing the way the person being broken up with hears them. For example when one person says, "I want to date around," the other person hears, "I want to see if I can find someone better." When one person says, "Let's just be friends," the other person hears, "Don't ever contact me again." When one person says, "You are too good for me," what the other person hears is, "I'm too good for you." When one person says, "It's not you; it's me," what the other person hears is, "It's not me; it's you." The examples were funny, until he got to one I had been on the receiving end of.

Leah chose to find her identity, value, and hope in the love of God. It took the rejection of a man to help her realize the love and acceptance of God.

Yes, love makes the world go round. In a sense, the Beatles were right — all you need is love. But it's a different love than most people expect. All we need is the love of God. He is the only one who can fill the void. When we feel that deep pang of loneliness, that's God crying out within us for fellowship. He wants to give us the love we have sought anywhere and everywhere else.

Paul says something to the church in Corinth that seems rather shocking to our modern ears. He encourages singles and widows to stay unmarried. Listen to his reasoning: "When you're unmarried, you're free to concentrate on simply pleasing the Master. Marriage involves … so many more demands on your attention. The time and energy that married people spend on caring for and nurturing each other, the unmarried can spend in becoming whole and holy instruments of God" (1 Cor. 7:32 – 34 MSG).

If you're not married you are able to have that much more time and commitment to give to God. Don't misunderstand; marriage is good. God isn't against it; in fact he's the one who came up with it. But as fantastic as human love is, it can never be a substitute for God's love.

The void in the human heart is God-shaped, not mate-shaped.

No Mistake

Looking back, Shannon could never remember pursuing God. What was clear was that God pursued her.

It was in her junior year that she met a teacher who was a dedicated follower of Christ. He let Shannon know that he was praying for her, and this led to conversations about God.

There was a spiritual void in her life, and she knew it. "I need something," she told him. "I need something in my life." And so he told her what it meant to find ultimate love and acceptance in Jesus Christ. "Come to church with my wife and me," he said. "We'll save you a place."

One Sunday she decided to test it out. She drove across town and found that even though she hadn't told them she was coming that weekend, the couple was waiting for her on the back row with a seat saved for whenever she decided to come. It felt amazing to be cared about this way. Afterward, at home, she cried out to God. "I don't know if you're real," she prayed. "I don't know if I accept all this stuff or not. But I need you! I need something!"

Shannon became a Christian, and she reached out to the church. For her the church turned out to be God's hospital where her wounds could be healed by him. She heard his voice saying to her what he says to you as well: You are not a mistake! I make no mistakes. In you I made a beautiful daughter whom I love passionately, completely, and eternally. Come to my arms and feel the forgiveness that is a forever thing. I have the love and tenderness you have always sought; I have the healing that your soul deeply needs.

If Shannon had never met Brian, just the love and acceptance of Christ would have been enough. She knew beyond any shadow of doubt that Jesus completed her. But as she surrendered her life fully to him, she discovered that God had other blessings in store.

Shannon and Brian dated for two-and-a-half years, during which time they agreed to abstain from physical affection; handholding and hugs were the limit. Brian understood that Shannon was working things out, and he was fine with this arrangement. "I just want to be with you," he said.

She found how sweet, how enriching the relationship between a man and a woman can really be when they are bound by the love and worship of the true God.

Idol ID

Are you disappointed in your love life?

If you're single, do you find that your life is somehow not complete because you haven't found that special someone?

If you're married, do find that your husband or wife is constantly disappointing you? Do you find yourself wondering if maybe you married the wrong person and your soul mate is still out there somewhere?

How you answer those questions reveals where you've

put your hope. And where you put your hope answers the question of what god you really worship.

Who do you sacrifice the most for?

Most of us could tell a story or two of the ways we have sacrificed to show our love to someone we had romantic feelings for. Certainly God calls us to love selflessly and sacrificially in our romantic relationships, but how do those sacrifices compare to the sacrifices you made in your relationship with God?

Think of an altar that represents your relationship with God. What are the sacrifices you've laid on that altar out of love for him?

Who is it that completes you?

Perhaps you have the challenge of a struggling marriage. Can the pain of that be keeping you away from God? Could you be living as Leah did, so focused on repairing what is damaged that you forget to praise and worship God? In the sad event that things don't improve, can you find satisfaction in God?

Perhaps you are single. Can you take Paul's challenge and give all the more of yourself to the kingdom of God? Sometimes we have to dethrone idols before we are ready for the blessings God has for us. Could it be that you're so focused on finding someone that you're not focused enough on becoming the person God wants you to be?

CHOOSING JESUS:

Jesus My Identity

*Idols are defeated not by being removed
but by being replaced.*

The god of romance came in and swept us off our feet. We fell head over heels for such a god. The music was playing. Our hearts were pounding. Our palms were sweating. Life was like a really corny, really wonderful movie that comes on TBS late at night.

We were in love with love, with the idea of a "soul mate," someone custom-made for us. The two of us would create our own world and lock everyone else out. We would complete each other's sentences, laugh at each other's jokes, and stare into one another's eyes.

But something went wrong. Once the giddiness wore off, we discovered that human beings are no more nor less than human beings. And ultimately human beings fall miserably short of being God.

No human being, we discovered, can meet all our needs. No human being deserves that much pressure. But Jesus can do it—Jesus our identity. It was wonderfully liberating to break free of the shackles of finding who we were in one person who could define for us what it meant to be alive. Jesus once said that no one has greater love than the one who will lay down his life for a friend. And then he proved it.

chapter 12

the god
of family

C. S. Lewis, the great British author of the *Chronicles of Narnia*, once boarded a bus for heaven.

He did this in imaginary form, of course, in a wonderful allegory called *The Great Divorce*. It's a book that examines why people choose for or against giving their lives to a full commitment to God. He shows that what we're doing is standing at the very gate of heaven and choosing between the eternal glory of God and the empty illusions of earth — what he calls "the great divorce" between heaven and earth.

In the book, Lewis climbs onto that bus with a group of fellow ghosts who have finished their earthly lives. They will be dropped off at a kind of way station in which they will make their decisions about eternity. (It's not as if salvation works this way, of course; the book is a kind of extended parable.)

For each newcomer, there is a bright, shining figure who steps out of heaven to receive his or her old friend, and to encourage them to make the full journey to heaven and the presence of God. These are not angels, but acquaintances from life who have been saved.

Pam is a woman who is disappointed to see that her younger brother, Reginald, is sent to greet her. She wanted it to be her departed son Michael, to whom she devoted her life.

Reginald explains that she isn't ready for that yet. She must first be eager to see God himself, then all the other wonderful blessings of heaven will be available. God isn't simply a way to get to heaven; heaven is a way to get to God, and Pam must approach it that way.

Reginald says, "I'm afraid the first step is a hard one. But after that, you'll go on like a house on fire ... when you learn to want someone else besides Michael."

Pam doesn't know what her younger brother is talking about. She says, "Well, never mind. I'll do whatever's necessary.... The sooner I begin it, the sooner they'll let me see my boy."

Reginald says that it can't begin with that kind of attitude. "You're treating God only as a means to Michael," he points out. She must learn to want God for his own sake. He can't come second in her affections; he can't even be tied for first.

"You exist as Michael's mother only because you first exist as God's creature," Reginald says. "That relation is older and closer." He goes on to explain to Pam that "human beings can't make one another really happy for long.... You can't love a fellow creature fully till you love God."

It becomes clear that Pam's love for her son was something of an obsession in life. After the boy died, she kept his room just as he left it for ten years. She neglected her other children, her husband, and her parents, to the pain and disappointment of them all. All of this was sacrificed on the altar of her adoration of her son.

"No one has a right to come between me and my son. Not even God," Pam declares. And it's very clear that this woman is so set on this view that she has chosen her own eternal destination.[27] In Lewis's view, it's not so much that God won't let us into heaven; it's that we won't let ourselves in. If we can't learn how to say, "Thy will be done," then finally God must sadly say, "Okay, then *thy* will be done."

Some people are uncomfortable with this little vignette. Shouldn't God give the woman credit for her powerful love? At least she loved *someone*; it just happened to be her own son. And what could be more noble than a mother's love for her own child? That's a *good* thing, not a bad thing, right?

The problem is that, as Reginald put it, the relationship with God must be recognized as "older and closer." The first commandment is to love the Lord our God, and the second is to love one another.

Picture it this way: Your life is a bicycle wheel. Every spoke in the wheel represents different and significant relationships that make up your life. One spoke represents mom. One spoke represents dad. One spoke represents a sibling. One spoke represents your spouse. One spoke represents a child, and on it goes. Our tendency is to make God a spoke in the wheel, but God isn't interested in being another spoke in the wheel of your life. God is to be the center hub that all the spokes come from and connect to. As T. S. Eliot put it, he is "the still point of the turning world."

Our relationship to the Father is more basic to who we are and to why we have been created. We are intended to love our children, parents, siblings, and spouses wholeheartedly, but always in the context of our primary, foundational love for God. Worship is for God alone. He must be our deepest love — actually the source of every other love. For only when we love God properly can we begin to love others properly.

According to the Ten Commandments, we are to *honor* our parents. But we are to *worship* only the Lord God.

That's what you might call a "top button" truth. Sometimes I'm in a hurry in the morning, and I button my shirt all wrong. Has this ever happened to you? Like everyone else, I take it from the top. I push that top button through the slot on the other side, except that, in my haste, I choose the wrong slot. I don't recognize my mistake until I get to the bottom and realize everything is out of line. If you get the top button right, then everything else tends to fall into place. If you get it wrong, then everything else is going to be out of alignment. You're going to look ridiculous.

God has ordered our lives in such a way that devotion to him is the top button. If that relationship is in proper order, then you're going to find that every other relationship, whether family or friend, is going to fall into place in a far more satisfying way. But if you're wrong on him, you'll get everything else wrong too.

This is why, in Lewis's allegory, the mother had to find her primary love for God before she could be allowed to see her son or anyone else in heaven. As things stood, she had made something beautiful — a mother's love for a child — into an ugly idol that distorted all her other relationships.

Augustine, the early Christian leader and writer, called these gods "disordered loves." He meant legitimate objects of love that have fallen as much out of order as a misbuttoned shirt.

As a matter of fact, it's precisely because a parent should love a child, a child should love a parent, and so on, that these relationships can be elevated to false gods. We're doing what we're supposed to be doing; we simply don't realize we've gotten things out of order.

"But I can't love my children any less," you might say. No, you can't, nor is that the message of this book, but you can love them *differently.* You can love them in the *context* of your primary devotion to God. And that, you will find, turns out to be a far greater, healthier, and more fruitful love.

The Test

One of the most harrowing stories in all of Scripture is found in Genesis 22. It follows the same lines as C. S. Lewis's story but has a much better ending. The story of Abraham and Isaac asks us this question: What if we were asked to prove that our love and commitment to God is greater than anything or anyone?

Abraham was destined to be a crucial figure in the history of humanity. He would be the first of a new nation, a nation that would be used by God to bless the world. When you lay down the foundation of an important building, one that will rise very tall, you test that foundation well. You make sure there will be no significant cracks. And God does this with his nation founder.

God tests Abraham in a couple of ways. One is to ask him to have faith in the promise that he and his wife will have a child, even in extreme old age, when they had not been able to have a child in their youth. When building a nation, God chooses the elderly barren couple, but would they believe?

After the promise is made nothing happens for a long time. Abraham and Sarah must believe for many years. They pass that test, and eventually Isaac, their son, is born.

This test turns out to be only the midterm. The final exam will take faith to another level entirely.

"Then God said, 'Take your son, your only son, whom you love — Isaac — and go to the region of Moriah. Sacrifice him there as a burnt offering on a mountain I will show you'" (Gen. 22:2).

"Your only son, whom you love." It's fascinating to me that this is the first time in the Bible the word *love* is used. The context is a beloved son who must be offered up as a sacrifice. That, of course, will become the theme of the Bible itself. The idea is first introduced right here, in Genesis, with the pivotal story of Abraham. The unity of the Bible never ceases to amaze me.

But what's important to realize is that God knew what he was asking. He wasn't some remote, cosmic deity who couldn't begin to understand what a man would feel over this request; God, who sees past, present, and future together, knew that he himself would make this same sacrifice of his one and only son whom he loved.

When we read this story in Genesis we are tipped off at the beginning that it's only a test. And we know that never in the Scriptures does God require that his people make a human sacrifice. He actually condemns the practice in several passages of Deuteronomy. But Deuteronomy hasn't been written yet and Abraham doesn't know this is a test.

It's also important to consider the love that Abraham and Sarah had for this child. They gave him a name that meant "laughter." After so many decades of waiting, there was such joy when he was born, such a sense of miracle to his birth. When a couple of strangers — angels in disguise — arrived to announce the birth, it was so shocking that Sarah burst out laughing on the spot. She was ninety years old and should have had great-grandchildren, but little ones had never been part of their life. Sarah laughed.

And then came the long wait, the doubts. What if it's all just a cruel joke? What if we're just getting old, imagining things? What if God had changed his mind?

When Isaac was born, what a day that must have been. How much laughter? How many tears and how much unbridled worship?

So there is a son. The couple loves him. They've stood holding hands in the doorway, watching him sleep at night. They've kept vigil when he caught a cold or a fever, pouring out prayers for his health. They've delighted as he learned to walk, to run, to speak, and now he is at the age where he begins to go out and help his father, a time that makes fathers swell up with pride.

But now, what a terrible, unthinkable blow falls — this abrupt command to lay that special, wonderful miracle child on the altar. To give him back.

The laughter turns to tears.

Greatest Gifts = Greatest Test

No parent in the world can hear the story of Abraham and Isaac without trembling. In stories, we become the characters. We identify with them. And in this one, Abraham is a Bible hero no one wants to be. We know what it's like to adore our children. Every child is a special, wonderful miracle child. We would give our lives for any of our own without even stopping to consider.

But we need to extend the parameters of this story. It's not just about children. Who do you love so fiercely, so protectively, so desperately? For whom would you lay down your life? A younger sibling? The parent you've always been closest to? Your spouse? It could even be a best friend; family can transcend blood, can't it?

God knows how DesiRae and I feel about our four children. There aren't words for it; fill in your own cliché here, but I can tell you it's a very deep and foundational thing with us. Yet we realize something kind of frightening: God's greatest gifts are also his greatest tests.

The more beautiful a thing is, the more capacity it has to become an idol. The more I fear losing it, the more likely I am to worship it. When God gives us a child he gives us a beautiful gift, and he says, "This is something I want you to have. I made it just for you. But can you love it without worshiping it? Can you keep it on its proper shelf? Can you love the gift in such a way that it makes you love the giver all the more?"

I have a wife I can never be good enough to deserve. God made her just for me — so I must guard my heart to keep loving her in the context of my worship of God and God alone. I suspect there's some person or thing in your life that is similar — the gift that is the test.

Abraham was a wealthy man, but God didn't test him there. Wealth, success, marriage — these things weren't disordered loves for him; if anything pulled Abraham's eyes from his Lord, it would be this child.

Verse 3 tells us that early the next morning, Abraham sets off for the very place where God sent him. If he struggles, if he debates within himself, he doesn't do so for long. He is up with the sunrise, preparing his mule, preparing his heart. I think he knew that the longer he delayed, the easier it would become to disobey.

Imagine the silence of Abraham as he leads his son and a couple of servants toward Moriah. It's a journey of several days, and it must feel like a funeral procession. No one else, of course, knows what's going on. They wonder why Abraham isn't his usual pleasant self.

Finally they can see Moriah off in the distance, and Abraham tells the servants, "We will worship and then we will come back to you" (Gen. 22:5).

He tells the servants to stay behind while he and his boy go to worship. Don't miss that word — *worship.* This is a meaningful point in the story. The presence of the word *worship*, right here at the moment of truth, tells us everything about Abraham's heart. In choosing God over everything and everyone else, he is defining what it means to worship.

The other word that stands out is *we.* "*We* will worship and then *we* will come back to you," Abraham says. But how exactly will "we" come back? Shouldn't he be saying, "*We* will worship and then *I* will come back to you"? In the New Testament we read of Abraham's faith and that he reasoned that God could raise his son from the dead. It's clear that he still fully trusts God. After all, God has promised a nation through this son.

The Bible tells us that they walked on together, and after a while, Isaac says, "Father?"

"Yes, my son?"

"The fire and wood are here, but where is the lamb for the burnt offering?"

"God himself will provide the lamb for the burnt offering, my son" (vv. 6 – 8).

And they continue to walk, until they come to the place God has described. Abraham builds the altar, arranges the wood, and then we can only wonder about his emotions as he binds his son where an animal should be. The account doesn't go into feelings; it deals only with firm obedience.

He reaches for the knife, and here, at the greatest moment of the test — the final one — he never falters until a voice from heaven stops him in his tracks: "Do not lay a hand on the boy," he said. "Do not do anything to him. Now I know that you fear God, because you have not withheld from me your son, your only son" (v. 12).

Is Isaac a disordered love for his father? No. The first commandment tells us we will have no other gods before God; the second says we will make no idols in the form of anything. Not even in the form of a beloved child.

WHO DO YOU LOVE?

In 2007, the Barna Group asked more than one thousand people to choose their most important relationship. Seven out of ten adults chose their earthly family over God.

Other findings:

- One out of three said their entire nuclear family is more important than God.
- Twenty-two percent named their spouse as the most important relationship in their lives.
- Seventeen percent placed their children in the top position.
- Three percent chose their parents.
- Only two percent named a specific friend as their most important relationship.
- Nineteen percent named God, Jesus Christ, the Trinity, or Allah as their top relationship. The most likely to make this designation were over forty in age.[*]

[*] Jennifer Riley, "Study: God Relationship Not Most Important to Americans," *Christian Post*, March 17, 2008, *www.christianpost.com/news/study-god-relationship-not-most-important-to-americans-31548/* (accessed October 4, 2012).

Abraham passes his test. He has shown the depth of his commitment to God, and that will enable him to love his son in the way God created him to — in an ordered way. He will not love his son any less for nearly having lost him; we can be sure that Isaac will be even more precious to him.

God has never and will never require a human sacrifice as an act of worship, but I wonder how you or I would fare. I wonder about the depth of our worship, our commitment to God. If you had to choose between the gift and the giver, who wins?

Disordered Loves

As I was working on this chapter, I happened to be talking to a young mother who listened carefully as I communicated these ideas. After taking time to reflect on it she became convicted that her children had become false gods in her life. I asked her what led her to that conclusion. She explained that it wasn't that she made them too much of a priority, she said; it was more about letting them control her. Her children, and what was going on with them, determined whether or not she had a good day. If they behaved themselves and didn't throw any tantrums, she could feel good about life. Otherwise she could not. If they were happy, she was happy. If they were upset, she was upset.

Her children had the power to fill her with anger or peace, with disappointment or joy. She realized that they were controlling who she was as a person and who she was becoming as time passed. This is exactly what a false god does: it recreates us in its own image.

It works this way: "People are slaves to whatever has mastered them" (2 Peter 2:19).

My friend wanted to be compelled only by the love of Christ, not the ups and downs of other people.

Do you have such a relationship? There's a funny old expression, "When Momma's not happy, ain't nobody happy." There may be a lot of truth to that, but when a family member consistently has control of our mindset and our emotions, it may be an indication that God is being replaced. In an earlier chapter, we discussed the way we begin to ascribe divine attributes to things that aren't divine: looking for satisfaction, significance, and ultimately even salvation in all the wrong places. God is jealous. He wants to provide those things, and he is the only one who can.

If the story of Abraham and Isaac is a troubling narrative, so is the statement of Jesus in Luke 14:26. It's another one of those passages we don't preach or teach too often. Jesus says, "If anyone comes to me and does not hate father and mother, wife and children, brothers and sisters — yes, even their own life — such a person cannot be my disciple."

This is a great example of a verse that cannot be taken out of context. We know from the full counsel of Scripture that we are to love our families. One of the commandments explicitly tells us to honor our parents, and we know Jesus would never contradict the law of God. So we dig a little deeper here and discover that in Jewish culture, *hate* was used to express a lesser form of love. The New Living Translation gets the idea of this verse when it says, "You must hate everyone else *by comparison.*"

So we're really not discussing any lack of love for family; we're discussing the centrality and the sheer magnitude of our love for God. This centrality is expressed as worship, and it can only be applied in one direction. God won't share the spot of centrality, the throne of your heart, with your spouse, your children, or your friends. You may not make for yourself an idol in the form of anything.

What happens when someone occupies the place in our heart that God should? Obviously, we hurt ourselves. My friend, whose children determined her state of mind, is one example. The woman in C. S. Lewis's story, who could not experience heaven because of the idol her son had become, is another.

But we also hurt other people. A relationship that is a disordered love and takes God's place in our lives is ultimately destructive to that relationship. Or put in the positive, we love others best when we love God most. Allow me to describe a few of the consequences of placing another human being on the throne of your heart.

Unrealistic Pressure

We touched on this in the last chapter, but let's come back to it for a moment. Have you ever considered the sheer pressure of asking someone to be God for you?

The phrase "He worships the ground she walks on" is not coincidental. The husband does this when he places his wife on a pedestal. She is his whole world, and if she is in a good mood, he is in one too. And soon she begins to feel the burden of responsibility for his happiness.

The doting wife simply feels she is maximizing her marriage, being the adoring wife. But when she crosses the line from proper to disordered love, and onward to idolatry, she places a terrible strain on the marriage. He can't have a bad day. He can't miss filling any need she has. If he does so, then it seems to her that the marriage isn't working. Maybe she moves from idolatry to adultery.

We're telling someone, "I'm placing all my happiness and well-being in your hands." And no one in their right mind would welcome such an arrangement, because they can't come through. The truth is that no human being can. Only God.

Unreachable Expectations

Children often feel the burden of living up to goals when the bar has been set out of reach. Consider the Little League player whose parents build their whole lives around his athletic experiences. This is a common theme in the suburbs. Parents get caught up in the thrill of favorably comparing their child to the children of their friends. Or perhaps they're living vicariously off their children's accomplishments.

The child feels this. Perhaps it's a bright daughter who could possibly earn a full scholarship to an elite university. Her parents are constantly reminding her, "You can't simply make good grades. You have to make the *best* grades. And have you joined enough organizations? Those look good for college admissions." Sometimes the child thinks, It wouldn't bother me so much to make a B. But it would kill my parents; they live for my report cards.

We live in the day of the "helicopter parents," so called because they hover over their children constantly. "My whole life is wrapped up in my kids," they smile, assuming this is a *good* thing. But it may actually be detrimental to their children leading healthy, ordinary lives. They can't all grow up to be president.

Those of us who counsel people see many adults who grew up believing they could never please their parents. Whatever they did, it was never enough. They are still out to try to make their mom or dad proud. The pressure they feel from mom and dad to meet their expectations has led to a life of insecurity. It seems they are always trying to hit a home run and bring home a perfect report card. Placing your value and finding your identity in your child puts the child in God's place in your life. And that's a lot to ask, even for an honor-roll student.

Unreasonable Disappointment

A friend of mine used to read comic books when he was a boy. There were ads for such things as x-ray specs and sea monkeys, amazingly wonderful things for only a buck or two. But he was particularly drooling over a set of a hundred fighting army men that came in a cool heavy-duty chest. The picture in the comic book was awe-inspiring: a great trunk, brass-trimmed with padlocks, that looked as if it had been carried across Iwo Jima and Guadalcanal. And it was packed with amazing toy soldiers in all kinds of fighting positions. He saved his two dollars and sent it off.

Six weeks for shipping and handling made for the longest wait of his life. He visualized two or three delivery men coming to the door, grunting under the strain of this incredibly cool war chest.

Then a little package came in the mail — a paper box about two inches by four inches, filled with ant-sized toy soldiers made of paper-thin green plastic, all of them the same. If you looked at them wrong, they'd break.

Even as a kid, he knew it was unreasonable to expect the amazing toys he visualized for only two dollars. He had a pretty good suspicion that those x-ray specs wouldn't really see through anything either.

Sometimes it's easier to understand that other things — money, pleasure — won't satisfy the soul. But family is different. We know that God ordained it, and it's the basis of society. So we tend to think we can create heaven simply by having a great family.

The deepest joy can come from only one source. As wonderful as marriage and parenting are, we must know that they won't be perfect, won't satisfy the soul. When we look to those relationships to do those things for us, we will inevitably be disappointed when the package is delivered.

Undeserved Criticism

My car ran out of gas a while back. I knew I was running low, yet I kept driving around, thinking the rates would drop a penny or two if I held out. Or maybe I would find that amazing service station that was stuck in a 1995 time warp in its pricing. Neither thing happened, so I was disgusted when the car wheezed to a stop. I climbed out to start walking.

I was angry. But I was angry at my car. I slammed its door to let it know how I felt. I kicked its tire to express my disappointment. How could the car do this to me? I know that's ridiculous, but we all have our irrational moments. It's irrational to expect a car to do what it was never designed to do. It's just as irrational to become upset at someone else for failing to give us a happiness and satisfaction that it's not in their power to give. I can't get critical of my car for not running without gas. It wasn't made to do that.

If I am constantly critical of others for the emptiness I feel, if I am always giving the ones I love a hard time for not meeting my needs and not making me happy, it's most likely because I'm asking them to do something they weren't made to do. They can give me love and joy, but there's a deeper satisfaction and contentment that must come from God alone. Criticism often marks our families and relationships because we want someone to do for us what only God can do for us and they are always falling short.

Unfair Comparisons

A final unintended consequence of disordered love comes when we begin to make unfair comparisons. I'm not happy in this marriage, someone thinks, but my friend is happy in his. It must be my wife's fault. I must be married to the wrong person.

And he begins to compare his wife to other women, always out of his frustration, always unfairly. It's unfair of course because he is looking to other women in social situations, at their very best, with the thought that maybe they could fill the emptiness.

When we set our hearts on our family, we make all of these mistakes, and we finally hurt our loved ones by holding them up to god standards. It's a terrible mistake that creates all kinds of resentful, bitter, and negative feelings in a spouse or a child.

Think about this. What if our loved ones somehow lived up to our high hopes? What if the daughter aced math? What if the wife did all the things her husband was demanding? Would anything be really different?

No, because the whole exercise began with a false premise: if X will only happen for me, then I will be satisfied. It's the thought that we can never quite conquer, the thought at the very heart of idolatry. If the daughter aced math, the parents would realize they still weren't satisfied, so they'd look until they found some other imperfection to work on or goal to accomplish. Once X happens, it is replaced by Y.

On the Altar

We can't expect things or people to fill a God-shaped void. So how should we look at our family relationships? Should we love less? Of course not. But we should love *differently.*

So what can you do? Should you go tell your spouse, "You're no longer what's most important to me?" Try whispering that sweet little nothing into their ear and see how that turns out for you. It doesn't sound like the key to a romantic evening. But here's the irony: taking those relationships off center and putting Jesus in his rightful place is the most loving thing we can do for those relationships. The supreme act of family love is to set your heart on Christ. Doing that leads to the most loving family relationships possible. Maybe what we ought to say is, "I love you too much to make you the center of my life."

When Jesus is truly my Lord, I am at my best as a husband, father, and friend. I place myself in a position to receive God's blessings in those relationships. So it is my prayer and desire to love my family enough to lay it on the altar of worship before God, with everything else that I have, everything else that I am. In other words, I want to do in spirit what Abraham did physically.

Oh, yes — there's a postscript to that story of Abraham. It shows the poetry and symmetry of history, when we look at things from God's perspective.

Abraham lived in Beersheba, a small oasis in the desert. God sent him on a three-day journey to Mount Moriah. That's quite a hike. Why would he do that?

After this story, one thousand years passed. According to 2 Chronicles 3, the king of Israel, David, bought a little acreage to build an altar and worship God. It was the place of Abraham's near sacrifice. And on that property, Solomon would finally build the great temple of Jerusalem.

Another thousand years passed. On this land, once again, a Father sacrificed his Son. This time it was no test. "He who did not spare his own Son, but gave him up for us all — how will he not also, along with him, graciously give us all things?" (Rom. 8:32).

What God asked of Abraham, but did not finally require, he was willing to do himself, for the love of you and me. He had a choice. On one side was his own beloved Son, sinless and perfect. On the other stand you and me, entangled in all the sin that makes us unworthy of his blessing. The only way we could be reconciled was by way of a sacrifice. And God so loved the world that he gave his only Son.

You are asked to choose God, to make him the source of our worship, but know this: he has already chosen you.

Idol ID

What person or people matter most to you in this world?

This is not a question you need to discuss with others. Just between you, your reflections, and God — who is it that you love so much that you'd lay down your life for them?

Those of us who are married would usually do this for a spouse. Those of us who are parents would nearly always do this for our children. And rightly so — it's a sign of deep and selfless love.

Take a moment to compare the sacrifices you are willing to make for that person with the sacrifices you have made to follow Jesus. Can you tell a story of how you personally sacrificed out of your commitment and devotion to Christ?

Is there a relationship in your life that seems to be the determining factor in whether or not you are happy and joyful or sad and depressed?

To what extent does this person, or persons, determine your state of mind?

To what extent have you organized your life around this relationship?

It's worth comparing the emotions you experience in worship. Though worship can be a quieter and more introspective experience, can you say that you experience feelings that approach the depth of what you experience with your family? Yeah, I know, it's a tough question.

The sources of our greatest and deepest emotional expression provide a strong clue to who or what controls us.

Can you find signs of "disordered love" in your family relationships? How would a deeper worship of God affect these symptoms?

Review the effects of disordered love near the end of

this chapter. Do you recognize these in your own family relationships?

Imagine your life as a fully devoted worshiper of God and follower of Jesus Christ. Envision yourself laying your family at the altar, along with every other part of you. You tell God, "I can't do this right. I worship you and you alone, and I trust you to make me the parent/spouse/child I need to be. I love these people deeply, but they will no longer be the meaning of my life. Only you will be. Help me be the person I need to be, so that you can bless these relationships. May these beautiful gifts from you make my heart more completely yours."

CHOOSING JESUS:

Jesus My Everything

*Idols are defeated not by being removed
but by being replaced.*

The god of family painted a beautiful picture. It showed a dinner table at Thanksgiving, with all the faces looking hungrily toward a baked turkey. Parents, children, and grandparents were all there, and it was so clear they loved one another.

Who wouldn't respond to such a scene? It's what we all want. The god of family may have been the most deceiving of all the false gods, because he seemed so decent and proper. He offered something that is already one of God's greatest gifts. But he offered a distorted version of it.

What he offered was not truly a family but a cocoon,

a place to shut the world out. He offered obsessive relationships, in which everyone must play god to someone else. He called all of it love, but in retrospect, it looked more like desperation. We doted on our children until we smothered them. We made demands of our marriages until we exhausted them.

Jesus showed us what family was supposed to be. He helped us understand that all of the relationships inside the home are reflections of what he is to us. It's the love of Christ that teaches us how to love each other. We said, "Family is everything," but it wasn't until Jesus was our everything that we discovered everything family can be.

chapter 13

the god
of me

I read a blog post the other day about a book published in 1964 called *The Three Christs of Ypsilanti*. The book was based on a psychiatric case study by Dr. Milton Rokeach, who was studying mental illness.

Rokeach was treating three patients at a psychiatric facility in Ypsilanti, Michigan. These patients, named Leon, Clyde, and Joseph, all suffered from delusions of grandeur, a common disorder. However each of these three men believed that they were actually Jesus Christ. You've heard of the "Messiah complex"? These three men took that to another level. The doctor worked hard at the task of introducing them to reality, but it was difficult to break through. In his book he tells about trying to convince these men that they really weren't God in the flesh.

For several years he had these three guys live together. They ate all their meals together. They slept in the same room together. Every afternoon they had a group therapy session together. Dr. Rokeach hoped that by spending time with others who thought they too were God would help reality set in. His approach led to some interesting conversations.

One of the men would say, "I'm the Messiah, the Son of God. I was sent here to save the earth."

"How do you know?" Rokeach would ask.

"God told me," the patient would invariably answer.

But just then, another of the three would interject, "I never told you any such thing!" And once the third got into the act, there was chaos. Once the disagreements became sharp and angry, each "Christ" would merely assume that the other two were simply patients in a mental hospital. He, on the other hand, was the genuine article.

Sadly Rokeach wasn't successful in his attempts to convince the men that they weren't God. They were trapped in this upside down reality where they thought they were the center of the universe and life was really all about them.

The foundation of reality is that there is one God, and you are not him. Once that's established, a choice must be made, and here it is:

I know that there is the Lord God, the master of all creation.

I also know there's the god of me, the pretender to the throne.

Whom will I serve?

In my brokenness, I feel the pull to worship me. I hear the whispered lie that Adam and Eve first heard: "Your eyes will be opened, and you will be like God" (Gen. 3:5). Why serve? You rule! You have everything you need to be your own god. Every day is a trip to that orchard; every day the snake is waiting. I must face this same choice: Will I worship God, and find my true place in this universe, the perfect place he has arranged for me? Or will I worship me and decide I can somehow come up with a better life than the Creator of all could design?

It's no coincidence that we've left this god, the god of me, for last. You'll confront many of the gods in our lineup at some point in your life. But this is one you'll grapple with every single day — multiple times per day.

Recognizing the God of Me

There are some symptoms that start to show up when the god of me edges himself onto the throne of my heart.

One symptom is arrogance. I'm always right. My way is the best way. The god of me won't listen to the wisdom of others.

This last Christmas we had opened presents at my in-laws' house. I was putting together one of the kids' toys on the family room floor and my father-in-law was sitting in his recliner watching the hunting channel — the channel that sends the message, "My son-in-law will never be a real man because he doesn't shoot things or build things." I don't know if he was more amused by the TV show or by the sight of me trying to put something together. I could feel the pressure mounting as I tried desperately to screw in a screw. It wouldn't catch the threading. My father-in-law said, "I think that's a reverse screw." I took that to mean that it screws in the other way. I was sure he was making this up in an attempt to further expose my wimpiness in front of my other male relatives. I was not going to be fooled. I knew the saying "righty tighty, lefty loosey." It's not "righty loosey, lefty tighty." I kept turning this screw to the right, certain that there was no such thing as a reverse screw and too proud to take the advice of my father-in-law.*

So let me ask you this. When was the last time you made one of the following statements: "I was wrong"; "You were right"; "I should have listened to you"; "I like your idea better"? Even when we don't realize it, a touch of arrogance may be present.

Another symptom that surfaces when I start to worship the god of me is insecurity. The god of me is consumed with what others think and terrified of trying something and failing. You can't help but be self-conscious, because when you're god, it's all about you.

How about defensiveness? Have you ever found yourself taking

---

* My editor says I need to finish this story. Whatever. I don't have to if I don't want to.

the slightest suggestion, the blandest criticism, as a personal attack? What makes people this way? Well, when you're god, you must be perfect, and no one else could possibly be in a position to criticize you.

The god of me will make you lonely, because you can't handle equals. You certainly can't handle authority. You need people who constantly reaffirm that it's all about you.

Listen to what God says: "In the pride of your heart you say, 'I am a god; I sit on the throne of a god' ... But you are a mere mortal and not a god, though you think you are as wise as a god" (Ezek. 28:2). The god of me is the most relentless idol of them all.

Gods at war? It's really me versus God. It's the flesh versus the spirit. All the other gods, in one way or another, take God off the throne and put me in his place.

THE U OF ME

A recent study by five psychologists suggests that today's college students tend to have more self-centeredness issues than those in the past.

From 1982 to 2006, 16,475 college students completed an evaluation called the Narcissistic Personality Inventory (NPI), a test that has been around for several decades. Narcissism is a term generally used to describe selfishness, conceit, or egotism, particularly in regard to how people relate socially.

Those tested must give rated responses to such statements as, "If I ruled the world, it would be a better place," "I think I am a special person," and "I can live my life the way I want to."

Scores have been spiraling in recent years. The study's leading author, Professor Jean Twenge of San Diego State University, believes we've gone overboard in telling our chil-

---

Broken Cisterns

It's an inescapable conclusion: worshiping the god of me is not in my best interests. The god of me takes many forms, but none of them satisfy. There is an image that is used in Scripture that captures what happens when I put myself on the throne of my heart instead of God.

In the Old Testament book of Jeremiah God speaks through the prophet Jeremiah and makes his case against his people. " 'Therefore I bring charges against you again,' declares the LORD.... 'My people have exchanged their glorious God for worthless idols. Be appalled at this, you heavens, and shudder with great horror,' declares the LORD. 'My people have committed two sins: They have forsaken me, the spring of living water, and have dug their own cisterns, broken cisterns that cannot hold water' " (Jer. 2:9, 11 – 13).

---

dren how special they are, when we should be showing them their responsibilities to others.

The study suggests that narcissists "are more likely to have romantic relationships that are short-lived, at risk for infidelity, lack emotional warmth, and to exhibit game-playing, dishonesty, and over-controlling and violent behaviors." Also, those with high scores on the inventory are more likely to cheat on tests.

The researchers believe that the self-esteem movement, beginning in the 1980s, has something to do with this trend. As an example, Twenge points to a version of the song "Frère Jacques" that is sung in some preschools now:

I am special, I am special;
Look at me, look at me![*]

---

[*] David Crary, "Study: College Students More Narcissistic," Associated Press, February 17, 2007.

He summarizes their rebellion into two sins: they have rejected him and have instead turned to worthless idols. He explains to the people that when we put ourselves on the throne instead of God, it's like insisting on digging our own broken cisterns to drink out of when there is a spring of fresh, living water flowing right beside us.

Cisterns were an important part of everyday life in Israel during Jeremiah's time. In fact, thousands of them have been uncovered by archaeologists. Rain was infrequent and scarce about half the year, so the people in those days would dig their cisterns and then line them with bricks and plaster to hold the water. But cisterns were always breaking and losing water. Even when they didn't break, the water would often become stagnant or the supply would be inadequate.

The people would have thought of Jeremiah's metaphor as ridiculous. No one would ever choose a cistern as their water source when a spring of crystal clear water was available. But that captures the ridiculousness of idolatry. We choose a broken well with stagnant water, instead of the spring of fresh water. We look to something or someone to do for us what God was meant to do for us.

Instead of looking to God as a source of comfort, we turn to food or mindless entertainment.

Instead of looking to God as our source of significance, we turn to our careers and our accomplishments.

Instead of looking to God as a source of security, we look to money and our investments.

Instead of looking to God as our source of joy, we look to our spouse and children.

Instead of looking to God as our source of hope, we look to politicians and legislation.

Instead of looking to God as our source of truth, we look to popular opinion and academic consensus.

Those things we look to for help aren't necessarily bad or evil in and of themselves. In fact God may use them to accomplish his purpose, but the question is, Have they become broken cisterns that we turn to instead of the living water? Am I putting my hope in something that doesn't hold water?

A New Hope

Over the summer my family house-sat for some friends while they were out of town. It had been miserably hot and we were excited about using the above-ground pool in their backyard.

The second morning we were there my wife woke me up and said the water level in the pool seemed a little bit low. She wondered if there might be a small leak. I went out to investigate. It was clear that the pool was slowly losing water from somewhere. I got in the pool and put on my son's goggles. They were quickly cutting off the circulation to my head so I knew I needed to find the leak fast. Eventually I located a hole about the size of a pencil eraser where the water was slowly leaking out.

I went to a pool store down the road and asked them what I should do. They sold me an underwater patch for the pool and explained how to use it. It seemed simple enough. When I got back to the house I followed the instructions. I applied the heavy duty glue to the patch, put on the goggles and swam down to apply the patch. When I started to press the patch against the side of the pool I watched in horror as the tiny hole slowly started to expand to the size of a basketball. Suddenly eighteen thousand gallons of water was rushing out and trying to push me through this hole.

I fought my way against the current and got out. In a panic I grabbed towels and tried to stuff them in the hole. The hole just got bigger. Finally I came to the realization that there was nothing I could do. I stood there in my goggles and watched helplessly as all the water emptied out of the pool into the back yard. My kids came out with stunned and disappointed looks on their faces. My youngest had tears in his eyes. One of my daughters looked at me and said what I was thinking: "Did that really just happen?"

That's a moment that many of us have experienced, metaphorically speaking. This is the inevitable moment of truth when you worship the god of me in all its forms. You watch all the water come rushing and, though you try desperately to contain it, there isn't anything you can do.

That's how some of you feel about your marriage. You were in love and you were sure it would be a happily-ever-after ending. You put your hope in your spouse. But you've been patching one leak after another and it seems that it is beyond repair.

That's how some of you feel about your children. You had such hopes and dreams for them. You've done your best and invested so much in them. And now there is a sense of panic as you see the decisions they are making and direction they are going and where it's all leading; you're left wondering, How did this happen?

That's how some of you feel about your finances. You were looking forward to that vacation or to retirement. But you've watched your savings and investments slowly drain away, and with it went your hope.

It's that moment when you realize that whatever it is that you've put your hope in doesn't hold water. With panic and dread you look on but it seems like there is nothing you can do.

Bruce Medes writes about a woman named Tammy Kramer, who was the chief of an outpatient AIDS clinic in Los Angeles County. One day she was at work when a patient came in for his daily dose of medication. He sat in tired silence on the clinic stool waiting for the doctor. Eventually the doctor, who was new to the clinic, came in and saw the patient for the first time. He administered the medication and then, just before walking away, the doctor said to the patient, "You know, don't you, that you're not long for this world? A year at most." Tammy Kramer said the patient came by her desk on the way out and she could see the pain in his face. He said through clenched teeth, "That S.O.B. took my hope away!"

Tammy Kramer said, "I guess he did. Maybe it's time to find another hope."

The god of me, in all its forms, always leaves you disappointed and disillusioned. So here's the question we're left with: Is there another hope? In Romans, Paul speaks of a hope that doesn't disappoint.

God longs for you to experience his living water. As he tells Jeremiah, the heavens look on with great horror at the sight of God's children drinking from the nasty cisterns and rejecting the fresh living water. It's one of the most heartbreaking things for God the father to watch. He has provided for and given his children what is pure and life-giving, and they are rejecting it. Imagine it this way: you take your kid out to eat at Ruth's Chris and you are going to order your child their first filet. It's brought to the table on a sizzling plate. Done to perfection. As a parent you can't help but smile at the thought of your child cutting into that steak and taking a bite. But let's imagine that when it's time to eat, your child reaches into their pants pocket and with their sweaty hand pulls out a piece of unwrapped, half-eaten beef jerky. It's got some mold on it as well as some lint from the pocket. Right in front of her is a perfect filet and she is chewing on old beef jerky. How would you respond? You would get upset. You've paid for the steak. You love your child. You want her to experience what you have for her. You would be both frustrated and saddened at the same time. That's how God feels when he sees his children reject his water for their own cisterns.

The Living Water

The "Living Water" is a title that Jesus gave himself in John 4. Jesus is traveling when the Bible tells us he "had to go through Samaria."

But if you look on a map, that doesn't seem entirely accurate. He didn't really *have* to go through Samaria. There were certainly ways around it. And most Jews would have done whatever was necessary to stay out of Samaria. There was a lot of prejudice between the Jews and Samaritans. But John says that Jesus *had* to go through.

There was a woman who lived there who had been desperately searching for something or someone to put her hope in, but time and again she had watched all the water rush out. Her search always ended in disappointment.

When Jesus arrives in Samaria he comes to a well. A well is different from a cistern. A cistern collects rain water, and a well allows you to draw water from underground. But as with cisterns, getting water from a well required a lot of effort. And like cisterns, wells would often be dry or full of stagnant water.

It's about noon when Jesus shows up at this well. It's the heat of the day and Jesus is no doubt tired from the walking. He sits down to rest at the well. He's thirsty, but there isn't much he can do about it because the well is likely around a hundred feet deep and he has no way to draw water from it. His disciples head off to grab some lunch at a nearby village but Jesus stays behind; he knew this woman would be coming soon.

When she arrives at the well to get water, Jesus says to her, "Would you give me a drink?" She does a double take and asks, "Why is it that you, being a Jew, would even speak to me?" And Jesus says to her, "If you knew who I was you'd ask me for water" (John 4:7 – 10, my paraphrase).

My guess is that at this point she thinks the sun must be getting to this guy. She points out to Jesus that he doesn't even have a bucket with which to draw the water. Jesus explains to her that if she drinks his water she'll never be thirsty again. He has something that will satisfy her thirst forever. She is thinking in terms of the physical world, that Jesus has physical water to quench her physical thirst. She has nothing to lose and so she agrees to drink this magical water from this strange stranger.

Jesus tells her to go back home and get her husband and then come back together. She tells him that she doesn't have a husband. Then Jesus, with a gentle smile, says, "You've spoken the truth. You've had five husbands and the man you're living with now is not your husband."

She realizes he's some kind of prophet and immediately tries to take the spotlight off of her by changing the subject. She asks a theological question. Jesus quickly answers it but she still doesn't understand. So she says in verse 25, "I know that Messiah (called Christ) is coming. When he comes, he will explain everything to us." She says to Jesus, "I know when Jesus comes he'll makes sense out of things."

Then in verse 26 Jesus says to her simply, "I, the one speaking to you — I am he." This is the only time we know of in his entire life that Jesus voluntarily revealed his identity. Imagine this moment for the woman. Her search had finally come to an end. Five husbands, that's five different wells, and all of them leaked. None of them held water for long. But when Jesus reveals who he is, there is something within her that knows he is the one her soul has been longing for.

We're not told her name. But I think I may have met her at church not long ago. I was visiting with a lady who shared with me how difficult life had been for her in recent years. She had gone through a divorce after being married for seventeen years. Because of the divorce she had lost everything and had been forced into bankruptcy. She had always taken care of herself physically, in fact less than two years ago she had run a marathon. But lately she has been dealing with painful arthritis in her joints that at times seems debilitating.

So much loss. But as she talked I was struck by her tone. She did not sound like a woman who was defeated and in despair. She went on to tell me how through all of this she had discovered a life in Jesus she never knew was possible before. She had spent countless hours digging cisterns. She kept digging at the cistern of marriage, the cistern of money, the cistern of health and fitness, hoping for a little satisfaction. None of them held water. And then, right when she felt she might die of thirst, she turned around to find right next to her a spring of living water. Here's how she explained it to me, "I didn't realize Jesus was what I really wanted until Jesus was all I had."

What Jesus says to this woman he also says to you and to me. "The water I give ... will become in them a spring of water welling up to eternal life" (John 4:14).

So what are you thirsty for? Are you stressed out and thirsty for peace? Are you lonely and thirsty for love? Are you bored and thirsty for purpose? Are you thirsty for acceptance? For validation? For significance? Are you just thirsty for something more? The god of me relentlessly calls us to chase after all these things. But ultimately we're left more thirsty than ever.

So here's the invitation from Jesus: "Drink from me, and you'll never thirst again."

notes

1. Tim Challies, *The Next Story: Life and Faith after the Digital Explosion* (Grand Rapids: Zondervan, 2011), 184.

2. Erwin Lutzer, *Managing Your Emotions* (Wheaton, IL: Victor Books, 1988), 109.

3. Michael Jordan and Mark Vancil, *Driven from Within* (New York: Atria, 2005), 110.

4. Paul Copan, *Is God a Moral Monster? Making Sense of the Old Testament God* (Grand Rapids: Baker Books, 2011), 35.

5. Paul Thompson, " 'My Body Is Only for My Husband': U.S. Christian Model Kylie Bisutti Quit Victoria's Secret Because It Clashed with Her Faith," *Daily Mail*, February 8, 2012, *www.dailymail.co.uk/femail/article-2097793/ Kylie-Bisutti-quit-Victorias-Secret-clashed-Christian-faith.html* (accessed September 28, 2012).

6. Edward F. Murphy, *Handbook for Spiritual Warfare* (Nashville: Thomas Nelson, 1996), 239.

7. *Nelson's New Illustrated Bible Dictionary*, ed. Ronald F. Youngblood, F. F. Bruce, and R. K. Harrison (Nashville: Thomas Nelson, 1995).

8. Gordon J. Wenham, *Genesis 1 – 15* (Waco, TX: Word, 1987), 226.

9. "Transcript: Tom Brady, Part 3," CBS News, *60 Minutes*, February 11, 2009, *www.cbsnews.com/2100-18560_162-1015331.html* (accessed June 11, 2012).

10. Derek Abma, "Men Think of Sex Only 19 Times a Day, Report Finds," *Vancouver Sun*, November 30, 2011.

11. M. Scott Vance, *The Chronicle of Higher Education*, quoted in *Christianity Today* 29, no. 18 (December 1, 1997).

12. "The Impact of Video Gaming and Facebook Addiction," *Anti Essays*, *www.antiessays.com/free-essays/130731.html* (accessed March 18, 2012).

13. Martin Lindstrom, *Brandwashed* (New York: Crown Business, 2011), 71 – 73.

14. Winifred Gallagher, *New: Understanding Our Need for Novelty and Change* (New York: Penguin, 2011), 126.

15. Robert J. Morgan, *Nelson's Complete Book of Stories, Illustrations, and Quotes* (Nashville: Thomas Nelson, 2000), 545.

16. C. S. Lewis, *Mere Christianity* (1952; San Francisco: HarperSanFrancisco, 2001), 135–36.

17. Aiden Wilson Tozer, *The Best of A. W. Tozer Book One* (Camp Hill, PA: WingSpread, 2007), 128.

18. D. R. W. Wood and I. Howard Marshall, *New Bible Dictionary*, 3rd ed. (Leicester, England: Downers Grove, IL: InterVarsity, 1996), 143.

19. Mark Twain, *Mark Twain at Your Fingertips: A Book of Quotations*, comp. and ed. Caroline Thomas Harnsberger (Mineola, NY: Dover, 2009), 525.

20. *http://www.princeton.edu/main/news/archive/S15/15/09S18/*.

21. Billy Graham, *Just As I Am* (New York: HarperCollins, 2007), 1190.

22. Thomas J. DeLong, "Why Chronic Comparing Spells Career Poison," *CNNMoney*, June 20, 2011, *management.fortune.cnn.com/2011/06/20/why-chronic-comparing-spells-career-poison/* (accessed October 2, 2012).

23. "Staying Alive, a Leadership Journal Forum," *Leadership* 23, no. 3 (Summer 2002).

24. Tony Campolo, *Who Switched the Price Tags?* (Nashville: Thomas Nelson, 2008), 26–27.

25. Patrick T. Reardon, "Lessons in Lust: Following Their Passion, Romance Novelists Go to School to Learn How to Write Hot, Sexy, and Spicy," *Chicago Tribune*, August 2, 1999.

26. See C. S. Lewis, *The Allegory of Love: A Study in Medieval Tradition* (Oxford, England: Clarendon, 1936).

27. C. S. Lewis, *The Great Divorce* (New York: HarperOne, 2009), 96–103.

not a fan.

chapter 1

D.T.R.

Are you a follower of Jesus?

I would say the chances are pretty good that you just skipped over that question. You may have read it, but I doubt it carried much weight or had any real impact. But would you let me ask you this question again? It's the most important question you will ever answer.

Are you a follower of Jesus?

I know, I know. You've been asked this question before. Because it's so familiar there is a tendency to dismiss it. Not because it makes you uncomfortable. Not because it's especially convicting. The question is dismissed mostly because it feels redundant and unnecessary.

Chances are that if you are reading this book you fall into one of two groups:

1. The "Jesus fish on the back of my car" group. You are serious enough about your faith that you shop in the Christian section of the bookstore. In which case, when I ask you *"Are you a follower of Jesus?"* it seems rhetorical and you're ready to put the book down, or at least go back and look at the table of contents to see if there is a chapter that might be helpful. You recognize that this is an important question for many to consider, but asking you? Well, it's like walking into a Boston pub and asking, "Who cheers for the Red Sox?" It's an important question, but you're so sure of your answer that your mind quickly dismisses it. You've already dealt with it. Asked and answered. But before you move on too quickly, let me clarify what I am not asking. I am not asking the following:

242

Do you go to church?

Are your parents or grandparents Christians?

Did you raise your hand at the end of a sermon one time?

Did you repeat a prayer after a preacher?

Did you walk forward during a twelve-minute version of "Just As I Am"?

Do you own three or more Bibles?

Have you ever appeared in a church directory?

Did you grow up going to VBS and/or church camp?

Is your ringtone a worship song?

When you pray are you able to utilize five or more synonyms for God?

I can keep going. Seriously, I can.

Have you ever worn "witness wear"?

Is the KJV the only real version of the Bible?

Have you ever kissed dating good-bye?

Under "religious views" does your Facebook page say "Christ follower"?

Did you dog *Harry Potter* and rave about *Lord of the Rings*?

Did you get a purpose driven life in 40 days or less?

Do you say "Bless their heart" before speaking badly about someone?

Do you understand phrases like "traveling mercies" and "sword drill"?

Here's my point: many of us are quick to say, "Yes, I'm a follower of Jesus," but I'm not sure we really understand what we are saying. To quote Inigo Montoya, "I do not think that means what you think it means."*

One of the most sobering passages of Scripture tells of a day when many who consider themselves to be followers of Jesus will be stunned to find out that he doesn't even recognize them. In the gospel of Matthew chapter 7 Jesus tells of a day where everyone who has ever lived will stand before God. On that day many who call themselves Christians and identify themselves as followers will stand confidently

---

*If you recognized this quote as being from *The Princess Bride* then give yourself an extra point. It's a favorite among Christians (even though Kirk Cameron isn't in it).

in front of Jesus only to hear him say, "I never knew you. Away from me." If you've just assumed you are a follower of Jesus, I pray that this book would either confirm that confidence or it would convict you to reevaluate your relationship with Jesus and reaffirm your commitment to follow him.

2. The "Why is there a fish on the back of my friend's car?" group. If you are a part of this group, then you likely didn't buy this book. In fact, you would never spend your own money on it. But somebody who cares about you, and who probably has a fish on their car, gave it to you. Because it was a friend or a relative you figured you would at least read the first chapter to be polite. And maybe you skipped over the question *Are you a follower of Jesus?* It's not that you're against the question or offended by it. It just doesn't seem relevant to you. But it's irrelevant to you in a different way than the people in group number one. It's not that you have already answered the question; it's that the question doesn't seem worth answering. You mean no offense; you're just not into it.

It doesn't bother you that some people choose to follow Jesus. That's cool, but it's not your thing. Kind of like your friend who's so into *Star Trek* that he asks you things like "ta' SoH taH HoD?" (That's Klingon for "Do you think Spock should be captain?"*) And you don't really care. If that's what he likes, fine. But you don't get the appeal.

But ... what if? Would you pause for a moment and ask yourself, *What if all of life comes down to this one question? What if there really is a heaven and there really is a hell, and where I spend eternity comes down to this one question?* That may seem completely ridiculous, but if there is some part of you that considers this a minute possibility, then isn't it worth thinking through that question? As you read this book I hope you would at least consider that this may be the most important question you ever answer. I believe that the reason we were put on this earth is to answer this one question. And the truth is, whether or not we do so consciously or intentionally, we all answer this question.

---

*Please note that I did not personally translate this nor do I speak a word of "Klingon." I do have a friend who speaks some Klingon. I ridicule and mock him, and I always do so in an actual language of real people.

I want you to know up front that I'm not here to "sell" Jesus. I'm not going to try and talk you into following Jesus by presenting the parts that are most appealing. Because here's the thing, and don't tell the people in group #1 I said this, but many of them assume they are followers of Jesus, but the truth is they have never heard the unedited version of what Jesus taught about following him.

My guess is that after reading this book there will be people in group 1 and group 2 that turn down the invitation to follow Jesus. After all, when we read in the Gospels about Jesus inviting people to follow him, some people signed up, but most decided to walk away.

Time for the D.T.R.

So where do you start in determining if you really are a follower of Jesus? How do you decide if this is even something you would want to consider? Let's begin by having a D.T.R. talk with Jesus. Some of you will recognize what the letters D.T.R. stand for. If you're not sure, let me give you a hint. For a young man involved in a romantic relationship, these letters are often enough to strike fear into his heart. He likely dreads the D.T.R. talk. In fact, many young men will postpone, run away from, and put off the D.T.R. for as long as possible. I have even known a few guys who have terminated the relationship when they sensed that the D.T.R. talk was imminent.*

Now do you want to guess what DTR stands for?

Define the Relationship.

This is the official talk that takes place at some point in a romantic relationship to determine the level of commitment. You want to see where things stand and find out if what you have is real.

In high school I went out on a first date with a girl that I really didn't know very well. We sat down in a booth at a restaurant and began the awkward first date conversation. During the appetizer I learned a

---

*True Story: One of my friends faked hyperventilating to get out of the D.T.R. talk. By "one of my friends" I mean me.

little bit about her family. While we enjoyed the main course she told me about her favorite movie. And then it happened. While we were eating our dessert she asked me, and I quote: *"Where do you see this relationship going?"* On the very first date she was trying to have the D.T.R. talk. I got out of there P.D.Q. That was the first and the last date.

I wasn't ready for that moment, but there comes a time when you need to define the relationship. It can be awkward. It can be uncomfortable. But eventually every healthy relationship reaches a point when the D.T.R. talk is needed. Is it casual or is it committed? Have things moved past infatuation and admiration and towards deeper devotion and dedication? You need to intentionally evaluate the state of the relationship and your level of commitment to the person.

So here's what I want to ask you to do. In your mind picture yourself walking into a local coffee shop. You grab a snack and get a drink and then walk towards the back where it isn't crowded and you find a seat at a small table. You take a sip of your drink and enjoy a few quiet minutes. Now, imagine that Jesus comes in and sits down next to you. You know it's him because of the blue sash. You're unsure what to say. In an awkward moment you try to break the silence by asking him to turn your drink into wine. He gives you the same look he used to give Peter. Before he has a chance to respond, you suddenly realize you haven't prayed for your food. You decide to say your prayer out loud, hoping that Jesus will be impressed. You start off okay, but understandably you get nervous and pray "Three things we pray: to love thee more dearly, to see thee more clearly, to follow thee more nearly, day, by day, by day." You quickly say "Amen" when you realize you're quoting Ben Stiller's prayer from *Meet the Parents*.

Before you have a chance to make things more awkward, Jesus skips past the small talk and gets right to the point. He looks you in the eye and says, "It's time we define this relationship." He wants to know how you feel about him. Is your relationship with Jesus exclusive? Is it just a casual weekend thing or has it moved past that? How would your relationship with him be defined? What exactly is your level of commitment?

Whether you've called yourself a Christian since childhood, or all of this is new to you, Jesus would clearly define what kind of relationship he wants to have with you. He wouldn't sugarcoat it or dress it up. He would tell you exactly what it means to follow him. As you're sitting in that coffee shop listening to Jesus give you the unedited version of what kind of relationship he wants with you, I can't help but wonder if that question, "Are you a follower of Jesus?" would be a little more challenging to answer.

It may seem that there are many followers of Jesus, but if they were honestly to define the relationship they have with him I am not sure it would be accurate to describe them as followers. It seems to me that there is a more suitable word to describe them. They are not *followers* of Jesus. They are *fans* of Jesus.

Here is the most basic definition of fan in the dictionary:

> *"An enthusiastic admirer"*

It's the guy who goes to the football game with no shirt and a painted chest. He sits in the stands and cheers for his team. He's got a signed jersey hanging on his wall at home and multiple bumper stickers on the back of his car. But he's never in the game. He never breaks a sweat or takes a hard hit in the open field. He knows all about the players and can rattle off their latest stats, but he doesn't know the players. He yells and cheers, but nothing is really required of him. There is no sacrifice he has to make. And the truth is, as excited as he seems, if the team he's cheering for starts to let him down and has a few off seasons, his passion will wane pretty quickly. After several losing seasons you can expect him to jump off the fan wagon and begin cheering for some other team. He is an enthusiastic admirer.

It's the woman who never misses the celebrity news shows. She always picks up the latest *People* magazine. She's a huge fan of some actress who is the latest Hollywood sensation. And this woman not only knows every movie this actress has been in, she knows what high school this actress went to. She knows the birthday of this actress, and she knows the name of her first boyfriend. She even knows what this actress's real hair color is, something the actress herself is no longer certain of. She knows everything there is to know. But she doesn't *know* the actress. She's a huge fan, but she's just a fan. She is an enthusiastic admirer.

And I think Jesus has a lot of fans these days. Fans who cheer for him when things are going well, but who walk away when it's a difficult season. Fans who sit safely in the stands cheering, but they know nothing of the sacrifice and pain of the field. Fans of Jesus who know all about him, but they don't *know* him.

But Jesus was never interested in having fans. When he defines what kind of relationship he wants, "Enthusiastic Admirer" isn't an option. My concern is that many of our churches in America have gone from being sanctuaries to becoming stadiums. And every week all the fans come to the stadium where they cheer for Jesus but have no interest in truly following him. The biggest threat to the church today is fans who call themselves Christians but aren't actually interested in following Christ. They want to be close enough to Jesus to get all the benefits, but not so close that it requires anything from them.

An Accurate Measurement

So Fan or Follower? The problem with asking that question of yourself is this: it's almost impossible to be objective. After all, if you say, "I'm a follower," what makes you so sure? What are the measurements that you use to define your relationship with Christ? Most would determine the answer to this question by using a highly subjective method of measurement.

Many fans mistakenly identify themselves as followers by using **cultural comparisons**. They look at the commitment level of others around them and feel like their relationship with Jesus is solid. Essentially they grade their relationship with Jesus on the curve, and as long as they are more spiritual than the next guy, they figure everything is fine. That's why some fans are almost glad when it's found out that the Christian family everyone admires has a child who rebels or a marriage that is struggling to stay together and isn't as perfect as it appeared. The curve just got set a little lower.

Have you noticed that when we compare ourselves to others as a way to measure our relationship with Christ we almost always put ourselves up against those who are spiritually anemic? I have a tendency to take this approach in measuring myself as a husband. I try and convince my wife how good she's got it by pointing to her friend whose husband never takes her on a date, or by telling her about my buddy who forgot his twenty-year anniversary. I've learned that when I start comparing myself to other husbands as a way to measure how I am doing as a husband, I am doing so out of conviction and guilt that I am actually not loving my wife the way I need to. If you find yourself measuring your relationship with Jesus by comparing yourself to others, that is likely a self-indictment.

Another measurement fans use is a religious ruler. They point to their observance of religious rules and rituals as evidence that they are really followers. After all, they reason, would a fan go to church every weekend, and put money in the offering, and volunteer in the nursery, and listen exclusively to Christian radio, and not see R-rated movies, and only drink a wine cooler at the party? *Hello? Of course I'm a follower. I'm not doing all that for nothing!*

We have other ways to determine if we are followers. Denominational measurements, our family heritage, and biblical knowledge are all ways we try to prove that we really are followers. But here's the real question: how does Jesus define what it means to follow him? Whatever measurement he gives is the one we should use.

Diagnosing Fandom

The Gospels record many examples of people having the D.T.R. talk with Jesus. In each encounter the person finds themselves in a position where the question "Fan or Follower?" has to be answered. Some are shown to be true followers; others are revealed to be nothing more than enthusiastic admirers. As we examine a number of these encounters, think of them as case studies that reveal different "symptoms" of being a fan.

With four kids at home, we are constantly on medical websites trying to diagnose whatever ailment is being passed around. One of my favorite websites has a search function that allows you to enter in whatever symptoms you suffer from and then it gives the most likely diagnosis. For example, if you type in "runny nose" and "nausea" the website informs you that it's likely the flu or a food allergy. If you add "lightheadedness" then it narrows it down to a food allergy. If you take away "lightheadedness" and add "fever," then the diagnosis is more likely to be the H1N1 flu.* The more specific the symptoms, the more likely you are to get an accurate diagnosis.

The biblical accounts of Jesus requiring people to define the relationship and honestly determine if they were true followers give us some telltale symptoms of being a fan. As we study these D.T.R. encounters with Jesus they will act as a mirror so we can have a more honest assessment of ourselves. Fans often confuse their admiration for devotion. They mistake their knowledge of Jesus for intimacy with Jesus. Fans assume their good intentions make up for their apathetic faith. Maybe you've already decided you're a follower and Not a Fan; well, I hope you keep reading, because one of the core symptoms of "fandom" is that fans almost always consider themselves to be followers.

So find a seat in the back of a coffee shop and read on. Let's honestly and biblically define the relationship. Are you a follower of Jesus? Or are you really just a fan?

---

*I have a difficult neighbor and have wondered if he has some kind of contributing health issue. I entered in "adult acne," "irritability," "halitosis," and "excessive body hair," but no results could be found. If you're part of the medical community I would appreciate your expertise in this matter.

Not a Fan

Becoming a Completely Committed Follower of Jesus

Kyle Idleman

Are you a follower of Jesus?

Don't answer too quickly.

In fact, you may want to read this book before you answer at all. Consider it a "define the relationship" conversation to determine exactly where you stand. You may indeed be a passionate, fully devoted follower of Jesus. Or you may be just a fan who admires Jesus but isn't ready to let him cramp your style. Then again, maybe you're not into Jesus, period.

In any case, don't take the question, Are you a follower of Jesus? lightly.

Some people don't know what they've said yes to, and other people don't realize what they've said no to, says Pastor Kyle Idleman. But Jesus is ready to clearly define the relationship he wants with his followers.

Not a Fan calls you to consider the demands and rewards of being a true disciple. With frankness sprinkled with humor, Idleman invites you to live the way Jesus lived, love the way Jesus loved, pray the way Jesus prayed, and never give up living for the one who gave his all for you.

Available in stores and online!

The Easter Experience

A unique, DVD-driven study. The Easter Experience brings the passion and resurrection of Jesus to life through dramatic storytelling and challenging teaching done in a highly cinematic style. Through these in-depth teachings, your small group will grow spiritually, bonding with each other as well as with the eternal message of Easter.

H2O: A Journey of Faith

H2O is a DVD-based, seven-week experience designed to create a safe atmosphere where people are comfortable considering the person of Jesus Christ. This creative, newly re-released tool meets an ancient need: sharing the truth of Jesus Christ through relationships and community. H2O transforms lives by feeding the mind, moving the heart, and stimulating the senses.

The Christmas Experience

A highly cinematic, video-driven study examining the Christmas story in detail, emphasizing how God chose each individual in the Christmas story for a specific purpose. Watch as Joseph leads his family with selfless faithfulness, as Mary follows obediently God's plan, and as shepherds struggle with doubt as they wonder...could this really be their Savior?

Share Your Thoughts

With the Author: Your comments will be forwarded to
the author when you send them to *zauthor@zondervan.com.*

With Zondervan: Submit your review of this book
by writing to *zreview@zondervan.com.*

Free Online Resources at
www.zondervan.com

Zondervan AuthorTracker: Be notified whenever your favorite
authors publish new books, go on tour, or post an update
about what's happening in their lives at www.zondervan.com/
authortracker.

Daily Bible Verses and Devotions: Enrich your life with daily
Bible verses or devotions that help you start every morning
focused on God. Visit www.zondervan.com/newsletters.

Free Email Publications: Sign up for newsletters on Christian
living, academic resources, church ministry, fiction, children's
resources, and more. Visit www.zondervan.com/newsletters.

Zondervan Bible Search: Find and compare Bible passages in
a variety of translations at www.zondervanbiblesearch.com.

Other Benefits: Register to receive online benefits like
coupons and special offers, or to participate in research.

ZONDERVAN.com/
AUTHOR**TRACKER**
follow your favorite authors